CHURCH HUMOUR

Judson K. Cornelius

ST PAULS

ST PAULS is an activity
of priests and brothers of the Society of St Paul
who proclaim the Gospel
through the media of social communication.

Printed by J. Njarakkatt at St Paul Press Training School.
Nagasandra, Bangalore and published by ST PAULS,
Bandra, Bombay 400 050.

1995

DEDICATION

Dedicated to the memory of my parents
at whose feet I learnt to love and laugh

And

to my grandchildren, Raja, Mona, Sunny, Bunty
and Monty who make my happy days happier
and my sour days, less sour.

CONTENTS

FOREWORD

Life is so filled with stress and strain that we could not possibly endure without some comic relief. I believe that the sublime and the ridiculous are not far apart. This is apparently what God wills. It is often said that anger takes far more energy than laughter. We could not possibly endure without comic relief. Can it be that humour is redemptive?

It is recorded that "Jesus wept." So he did. Some go so far as to say that he did not laugh. This can hardly be true. He must have shown great good humour at times. He was so loved by ordinary people that he must have laughed as well as wept. Some of his figures of speech must have been deliberately framed to evoke laughter. So it was that the people heard him gladly. Some of his parables must have evoked laughter. Moreover, the children loved him.

We are in debt to Judson K. Cornelius for this collection. Laughter is a gift of God and so is the power to call it forth. Laughter is good medicine; moreover, it is free. May God bless those who read this volume and bless also the one who brought it together.

— James K. Mathews

Albany Area
The United Methodist Church,
235 Lark Street, Albany,
NY 12210-1108, U.S.A.

PREFACE

This book is a labour of love to me. My object in doing this book is not only to show how much humour there is in Christian life but also to highlight the fact that a sense of humour can help one overlook the unattractive, tolerate the unpleasant, cope with the unexpected and smile through the unbearable. This volume does not make any scholarly pretentions and is a compilation of amusing jokes, anecdotes, verses, puns, quips, quotes, spoonerisms etc. Sacrilege, crudity and unsocial uproars find no place in this book.

Several Church dignitaries, famous humorists, renowned scholars, friends, well wishers and members of my family have helped me in the compilation of this volume. My principal obligations are to Lord Robert Alexander Kennedy Runcie, former Archbishop of Canterbury and presently Member of the House of Lords, Rt. Rev. Graham Douglas Leonard, former Bishop of London, Rt. Rev. Richard Harris, Bishop of Oxford, Rev. Leslie B. Flynn, Pastor Emeritus and author of more than thirty books, Rev. Tal D. Bonham, author and executive Director-Treasurer, State Convention of Baptists in Ohio, Larry Wilde America's Best-selling humorist, Kariel Gardosh (Dosh), famous humorist of Israel, Prof. Itzhak Galnoor of Hebrew University, Jerusalem, Prof. Steven Lukes, Oxford University, Dr. Raleigh H. Pickard of Penny Farm, Florida, Dr. Nelson Samuel, M. Vittal, Y. Samuel, S. James, Rev. Manick Samuel, Rev. Patrick Forbes, Ms Elizabeth Gnasso of Prentice-Hall Inc, New Jersey, Most Rev. Dr. Mar Aprem and many other friends for sending material for the book; to most Rev. John Stapylton Hobsgood, Archbishop of York, Rt. Rev. David Edward Jenkins, Bishop of Durham, Bishop M. Elia Peter, Bishop S.K. Parmar, Bishop S.K. Samuel, Bishop B. James, Rev. K.D. Bhasker and Miss Ratna Seshappa for their encouragement, good wishes and prayers without which I should have attempted little and achieved still less; to the General Board of Global Ministries, The United Methodist Church, New York, my brother, D.C. Kavoori, and my daughter, Priyadarshini for their munificent financial help; to Mr V. Ganeshan and my daughter, Sumathi Pamela for typing and retyping the several drafts of the manuscript with meticulous care and mathematical neatness; to my wife, Manikyam and my daughter-in-law, Nalini Antoinette for going through the manuscript with commendable thoroughness; to Bishop James K. Mathews for writing a brief but beautiful foreword; to my publishers for making the book so elegant and attractive and to the two brilliant reconteurs of stories, T. David and G. Simon for unceasingly strengthening my resolve to bring out the book.

I am sure, in the following 35 chapters, you will enjoy reading scores of jokes, anecdotes, limericks, puns, spoonerisms, verses, etc., as much as I have enjoyed collecting them from all over the world.

And best wishes for lots and lots of laughs!

Judson K. Cornelius

Hyderabad, India

1
ABSENT-MINDED CLERGYMEN

1. Three absent-minded clergymen, one of whom was a bishop of bountiful proportions, were talking about the controversial views of David E. Jenkins, Bishop of Durham, and James A. Pike, former Episcopal Bishop of California, in a railway station. They got so interested in what they were discussing that they didn't notice the arrival of the train. As the train whistled for departure, they got puzzled and ran for the train. The two ministers managed to get into the train, but the bishop couldn't make it. As he stood helplessly watching the train disappear into the distance, a man tried to cheer him up, saying "You shouldn't feel too bad. Two out of three made it, and that's a good average." The portly bishop grinned sheepishly and said, "But they came to see me off."

☆

2. Rev. Simple Simon once drove his car into another at a cross-roads. His was not damaged, but the stranger's car was crushed.

"Ring me up and tell me how much the repairs cost. I'll pay the bill," he told the stranger and started to drive away.

"What's your phone number?"

"It's in the telephone directory," the man of the cloth called back.

"What is your name?"

"Oh, it's in the telephone directory, too!"

☆

3. An absent-minded clergyman was standing in a bus, holding on to the rail with one hand while his other hand clutched a Holy Bible. Seeing restlessness in the face of the clergyman, a sympathetic fellow-traveller said, "Is there anything I can do to help you, parson?"

"Why, yes, there is, if you don't mind," said the distrait minister. "Would you mind, please hold on to the rail so that I can get my bus fare out?"

7

4. The forgetful pastor looked anxiously round the vestry, after Sunday service, and asked the associate pastor, "Did you see where I put my gown?"

"You have it on, reverend."

"Thank you very much for telling me. Otherwise I might have gone off without it."

☆

5. The great Rev William Archibald Spooner was notorious for his absent-mindedness. Once he preached for half an hour on the admonitions of Aristotle, only to realise at the end of his Sermon that he had used a wrong name throughout. The sermon was on the admonitions of St Paul. Apologizing to his perplexed congregation at the end of the discourse, he begged them to remember the theology that he had explained but to forget the name he had used.

Once Rev Spooner had an appointment with a parishioner and so he went to meet him at the Dulman in Greenwich. Only after a long day of fruitful searching did he recall that the meeting was to have taken place at Greenman in Dulwich.

This great divine found time now and then to indulge in some queer behaviour. Once a lady parishioner after a visit was leaving his dim-lit quarters. Spooner said to her, "I will come and turn on the other lights, and see you safely down the stairs," whereupon he proceeded to turn out the only light that burned over the stair case and led the visitor in total darkness.

There is another interesting story about him. One day he went to a junior colleague and invited him to have lunch with him the following Sunday and meet the newly elected fellow, Stanley Casson.

"But Dr Spooner, I am Stanley Casson," said the junior colleague. "So what?" said the legendary clergyman, "come all the same."

☆

6. Distrait Parson (leaving the church): Who's the absent-minded one now? You left your unbrella back there and I not only remembered mine, but brought yours too."

Wife (gazing blankly at him): But neither of us brought one to church.

7. Michael Ramsey was, perhaps, the most absent-minded Archbishop of Canterbury. The landlady of a house where he was a paying-guest as a young curate recalls hearing a knock at the door one day as she was cleaning up the room. Presuming it was someone seeking the curate, she called out, "Mr Ramsey has gone out."

"Thank you very much for the information," said the absent-minded curate.

The landlady realised the voice was that of her lodger. She reached the door just as he was turning away.

☆

8. Bishop Gilbert Burnet was notorious for his absent-mindedness. Driving in a horse carriage with the Duchess of Marlborough, after her husband's disgrace, he likened this general to Belisarius.

"But," said the Duchess eagerly, "How come it that such a great warrior was so miserably and universally discredited?"

"Oh, madam," exclaimed the distrait prelate, "He had such a brimstone of a wife!"

☆

9. The gloomy Archbishop Temple resigned the See of Dublin on grounds of ill-health and old age and settled in London. Once he and his wife visited Dublin and stayed with Archbishop Lord Trunket as his guests. Sitting in his old chair in the dining hall, he lapsed in memory and looking at his wife, remarked, "I am afraid, my dear, that we must put this cook among our failures."

☆

10. Invited to give a devotional talk on Daniel at the Couples' Club, a young Churchman had trouble remembering the names of Daniel's three friends who were thrown into the fiery furnace, Shadrach, Meshach and Abednego. So he decided to write them on the inside of his suit jacket.

Sure enough as it came time in his devotional to name Daniel's three friends, his mind went blank. Looking inside his jacket, he blurted out: "Hart, Schaffner and Marx."

☆

11. A woman was sitting in a cafe when a clergyman and his wife entered and sat down at the next table.

9

After a while the clergyman went out and bought a paper. He came back so deeply engrossed in it that he didn't notice he had taken his seat at the wrong table, where the woman sat.

Still not realising his error and still enthralled in the paper he said, "Well, my dear, what are we going to eat?"

The woman was so astonished that she could not reply, and the clergyman receiving no answer, peeped above his paper. Seeing his error, he said, "Oh, I'm sorry. Wrong wife!"

2
ADAM AND EVE

1. Adam and Eve had many advantages, but the principal one was that they escaped teething.

☆

2. The only man in history who never looked at other women was Adam.

☆

3. Probably no man got so much conversation out of a surgical operation as Adam did.

☆

4. I wish Adam had died with all his ribs intact!

☆

5. Adam, they say, was a happy man because he had no mother-in-law.

☆

6. The story of Adam and Eve takes a lot of believing. It's probably just a rib.

☆

7. As soon as Eve ate the apple of Wisdom, she reached for the fig leaf.

☆

8. The Bible says that the last thing God made was Eve. He must have made her on a Saturday night — it shows fatigue.

☆

9. Surely God must have been disappointed in Adam; He made Eve so different.

☆

10. While Adam slept, Eve from his side arose,
Strange, his first sleep should be his last repose.

11. Devil was more generous than Adam,
    That never laid the fault upon his madam,
    But like a gallant and heroic self,
    Took freely all the crime upon himself.

☆

12. After several days' absence from the Garden of Eden, Adam returned to find the lonely Eve sulking and suspicious of his actions. "Really, now darling," said Adam, "How could you possibly be jealous of me? Don't you realize that I am the first man and you're the first woman — the only two humans in existence? There just aren't any others."

"Yes, I know," replied Eve. "Still..."

Adam was finally able to soothe his wife and soon they both drifted off to sleep. In the midst of the wee dark hours of morning, Eve arose from her sleep, pulled the bearskin covering off Adam and then counted his ribs!

☆

13. There was a dear lady of Eden,
    Who on apples was quite fond of feedin'
    She gave one to Adam
    Who said, "Thank you, Madam,"
    And then both skedaddled from Eden.

☆

14. In the Garden of Eden sat Adam,
    Disporting himself with his madam,
        She was filled with elation,
        For in all of creation,
    There was only one man—and she had'm.

☆

15. An Englishman, a Frenchman and a Russian were arguing about the nationality of Adam and Eve.

"They must have been English," declares the Englishman. "Only a gentleman would share his last apple with a woman."

"They were undoubtedly French," says the Frenchman. "Who else could seduce a woman so easily?"

"I think they were Russians," says the Russian. "After all, who else could walk stark naked, feed on one apple between the two of them and think they are in Paradise?"

12

16. In Genesis, Adam's the winner,
    Whilst Eve is denounced as the sinner
        For the fruit she brings;
        That's how men see things!
    He blames HER when she brings his dinner.

☆

17. When Eve upon the first man
    The apple pressed, with specious cant,
    Oh! What a thousand pities then
    That Adam was not adamant.

☆

18. When Eve brought woe to all mankind,
    Old Adam called her woe man,
    But when she woo'd with love so kind,
    He then pronounced her woman.

☆

19. When Adam, waking first his lids unfolds,
    in Eden's groves, beside him he beholds
    Bone of his bone, flesh of his flesh, and knows,
    His earliest sleep has proved his last repose.

☆

20. After the fall in the Garden of Eden, Adam was walking with his sons, Cain and Abel. They passed by the ruins of the Garden of Eden. One of the boys asked, "What is that?"

Adam replied, "Boys, that's where your mother ate us out of house and home."

☆

21. The story of Adam and Eve was being carefully explained in the children's Sunday School Class. Following the story, the children were asked to draw some picture that would illustrate the story.

Little Fred was most interested and drew a picture of a car with three people in it. In the front seat, behind the wheel was a man and in the back seat, a man and a woman.

The teacher was at a loss to understand how this illustrated the lesson of Adam and Eve.

13

But Fred was prompt with his explanation. "Why, this is God driving Adam and Eve out of the garden!"

☆

22. WHEN ADAM WAS FIRST CREATED

When Adam was first created,
And Lord of the Universe crowned,
His happiness was not completed,
until that a helpmate was found.
He had all things in food that were wanting
To keep and support him in life,
He'd horses and foxes for hunting,
Which some men love more than a wife.

He'd a garden so planted by nature
Man cannot produce in his life,
But yet the all-wise Creator,
Still saw that he wanted a wife.
Then Adam he lay in a slumber,
And there he lost part of his side,
And when he awoke, with a wonder,
He beheld his most beautiful bride.

In transport he gazed upon her,
His happiness now was complete,
He praised his most beautiful donor
Who had thus bestowed him a mate
She was not took out of his head, Sir,
To reign or to triumph over man;
Nor was she took out of his feet, Sir,
By man to be trampled upon.

But she was took out of his side, Sir,
His equal and partner to be,
But as they're united in one, Sir,
The man is the top of the tree.
Then let not the fair be
By man, as she's part of himself,
For woman by Adam was prized
More than the whole world full of wealth.

14

Man without woman's a beggar,
Suppose the whole world he possessed;
and the beggar that's got a good woman,
With more than the world is he blest,
When Adam was first created
And Lord of the universe crowned,
His happiness was not completed,
Until that helpmate was found.

3
ARCHBISHOPS

1. I am beholden to the Archbishop of Canterbury, Robert Alexander Kennedy Runcie, for sending me this amusing piece. He says that he is particularly fond of a border sign that he saw on the road between Jerusalem and Damascus saying 'double-crossing only permitted to diplomats and certain bishops!'

☆

2. Desmond Tutu, Bishop of Johannesburg (now Archbishop of Cape Town), in South Africa, and winner of 1984 Nobel Peace Prize, leads the war against apartheid. His puckish wit and gentle manner captivate audiences worldwide. At an ecumenical service in New York, in November 1984, he demonstrated his deft use of humour.

"When the missionaries first came to Africa," he said, "they had the Bible and we had the land. They said, 'Let us pray.' We closed our eyes. When we opened them the tables had been turned, we had the Bible and they had the land."

☆

3. Even the Archbishop of Canterbury has to deal with impertinent people occasionally. The venerated prelate was giving a talk, in London, in the course of which he observed: "It is said that the road to hell is paved with good intentions. But these days, it seems to me, it is paved with wine, women and motor cars."

Voice from the crowd, "Then the sting of death is gone!"

Thanks to this Archbishop, England has been spared a certain amount of scenery desecration. He it was who initiated a campaign against advertising signs. This was aided by such slogans as 'I think that I shall see a road-sign as a tree.' And the Archbishop penned a little verse which also helped. Referring to those who, for commercial reasons, ruin the aesthetic pleasures of others, he wrote:

THEY PLAY ABOUT WITH WORKS OF GOD,
AND MAKE THEM SEEM UNCOMMON ODD.

4. Archbishop Temple was staying with a lady who used to rise early and prepare breakfast for her family and guests. On waking, he heard a voice singing, "Nearer, my God to thee" and reflected on the exemplary piety of his hostess. At breakfast that morning, he told her how pleased he was and she was just a little embarrassed. "That's the hymn I boil the eggs," she confessed. "Three verses for soft and five for hard."

☆

5. A certain prince, who was at the same time Archbishop, had one day made use of blasphemous words and then said to a farmer, who could not hide his astonishment: "Why do you look so astonished?"

The farmer replied, "Because an archbishop can be so irreverent."

"I do not swear as an archbishop," replied the archbishop, "but as a prince."

"But, Your Highness," answered the farmer, "when the prince goes to hell what will become of the archbishop?"

☆

6. A man once ran into an Archbishop on the streets of Baltimore. He remembered that somewhere he had met the prelate but what his name was, he could not recall. "Now, where in hell have I seen you?"

"From where in hell do you come, Sir," retorted the waspish archbishop.

☆

7. George Moore, while breathing the rarefied air on the upper slopes — if not the summit — of Parnassus, was like many ordinary mortals in that he had a rather large streak of vanity. This vanity led him on one occasion during his Enfant Terrible days in Dublin, to send the following letter to the Most Rev. Dr Walsh:-

"My dear Archbishop, Have you heard the news? I have left the Church — George Moore."

Back came the reply which set all Dublin tittering, and which members of all sects regarded as a sort of minor triumph for Christianity. It read:-

17

"My dear George Moore, have you heard the story of the fly on the end of the cow's tail? The fly said, 'Cow, I am about to leave you.' The cow looked over her shoulder at the tip of her tail and said, "Oh, really? Why I didn't know you were there! — William, Archbishop of Dublin."

☆

8. While on the subject of errors in introductions, there was the occasion when the Bishop of London was mistakenly called the Archbishop of Canterbury at a function which he was about to address. This would not have mattered had not the Archbishop himself been on the platform and was also to speak.

The Bishop handled the situation with calculated charm. He put a hushing finger to his lips, saying. "Not yet! Not yet."

☆

9. When Archbishop Roncalli was Nuncio to France, he had invited a few friends to dinner. The Deputy Prime Minister of France was the first guest to arrive. On seeing him, Archbishop Roncalli exclaimed, "My God! I had forgotten!" But he promptly brought out a couple of aprons, and he and the Deputy Prime Minister of France were busy preparing the meal.

☆

10. A woman told Archbishop Temple about the miraculous escape of her aunt from certain death. Apparently, her aunt was about to leave on a sea voyage when she had a terrifying dream — the boat sank with all hands on board. She had the same dream twice and abandoned her trip. True to her premonition, the vessel sank with a terrible loss of life.

"Now don't you consider, Archbishop," said the woman, "that it was a remarkable interposition of providence to save my aunty?"

"Well, ma'am," replied Temple, "as I don't know your aunt, I can't say."

☆

11. When Rt Rev. Michael Ramsey, the hundredth Archbishop of Canterbury was attending a function in New York,

a photographer trying to get his attention, coudn't think how to address the prelate. In desperation, he said, "Archie, would you mind turning your head this way, please?"

His Eminence turned his head and as gentle and kindly as ever, said, "Gentleman, my name is not Archie. It's Mike."

☆

12. An aging archbishop had a presentiment that he would fall a victim to a paralytic stroke. One evening, while he was playing chess with a fascinating lady, he suddenly felt that he had a stroke and fell back in his chair, murmuring, "Your move."

Frightened, the lady hurried to his side and asked, "Are you ill, Your Grace?"

"It has come," the archbishop replied. "At last it has come. My right side is paralysed."

"How can you be so certain?"

"I have been pinching my leg," said the archbishop weakly, "and there is absolutely no feeling."

"Oh," said the fascinating lady, blushing, "Your Grace, kindly pardon me. But it was my leg you were pinching."

☆

13. Once Winston S. Churchill, along with his Defence Minister, Harold Macmillan, was flying to Cyprus to meet Archbishop Makarios for the first time. Churchill turned to Macmillan, and said, "What type of man is this Makarios? Is he one of those austere, God-fearing men, concerned more with heavenly rewards or is he one of those wily, intriguing prelates concerned rather with worldly gain?"

"Annoyingly, Winston," said Macmillan, "the Archbishop seems to be one of the latter."

"That's fine," said Churchill, "then he is one of my kind and I can get along with him."

4
BAPTISMS

1. An Anglican curate in want
   of a second-hand portable font
      Will exchange for the same
      A photo (with frame)
   Of the Bishop Elect of Vermont.

☆

2. The parents of eighteen or nineteen children took their latest to be christened, having decided upon the name 'Fred'. The following day the harassed husband visited the priest and asked if it would be possible to change the baby's name, from Fred to Sydney.

"But why do you wish to change the infant's name?" demanded the priest.

"Last night," explained the husband, "we suddenly remembered we already have a Fred."

☆

3. Aged Negro Preacher: There will be a baptism in the church on Sabbath. Two adults and six adulteresses, going to be baptised.

☆

4. The family gathered around the baptismal font and the ceremony commenced.

"And now," said the priest, "what name are you giving the child?"

"Peter Xavier Timothy Eammon Richard Albert Daniel Sean Paxton," announced the grandmother.

The priest turned to the altar boy, "Quick, get more Holy Water."

☆

5. The two American ministers travelling in Germany decided to go to church. Knowing no German, they figured to

20

play safe by picking out a dignified-looking gentleman sitting in front of them and doing whatever he did.

During the service the pastor made a special announcement, and the man in front rose. The two Americans rose quickly only to be met by roars of laughter.

When the service was over, they discovered the pastor spoke English and asked what the cause of the merriment had been.

"Oh," said the pastor, "I was announcing a baptism and asked the father of the child to stand."

☆

6. A spry old party of eighty suddenly decided to marry a blond and avaricious maid of seventeen. The clergyman took one look at the pair, and observed "The font is at the other end of the church."

"What do I want with the font?" queried the old gent.

"Oh, I beg your pardon," said the clergyman, with a straight face, "I thought you had brought your grandchild to be christened."

☆

7. A Presbyterian and a Baptist minister were discussing baptism. After a beautiful dissertation on the subject by the Baptist Minister, the Presbyterian minister asked if the Baptist considered a person baptised if he were immersed in water upto the chin. "No," said the Baptist.

"Is he considered baptised if he is immersed up to his nose?" asked the Presbyterian.

Again the Baptist's answer was, "No."

"Well, if you immerse him up to his eyebrows, do you consider him baptised?" asked the Presbyterian.

"You don't seem to understand," said the Baptist. "He must be immersed completely in water until his head is covered."

"That's what I've been trying to tell you all along," said the Presbyterian. "it's only a little water on the top of the head that counts."

21

8. There was great rejoicing in church circles of a town in Arkansas when the leading reprobate and liar of the county announced that he had seen the light and desired to be baptised. They doused him in the icy waters of the creek while all the town watched and applauded. As he came up with his teeth chattering, a friend hollered "Hey, Tom, that water cold?"

"No, Sir," the prodigal son cried bravely.

"Better duck him again, Parson," advised the friend. "He ain't quit lying yet."

☆

9. Deacon Jones was deaf; but he was as energetic as they make 'em. His particular function in the Log City Presbyterian Church was selling the new hymnals to the members at seventy-five cents a copy.

One day, after the preacher finished his sermon, he arose and said, "All you who have children to baptise will please present them next Sabbath."

Deaf Deacon Jones, anxious to be of assistance, and supposing the announcement concerned the hymnals, rose and cried out: "All you who haven't can get as many as you want by calling on me, at seventy-five apiece."

☆

10. Despite his (Sir Arthur Conan Doyle's) macabre interest in Communication with the dead, he was always full of fun. He spent considerable money and even sacrificed his reputation to some extent in order to promote his spiritualistic beliefs. At a meeting where he was expounding his views on the subject a number of reporters were seated almost under his lectern.

With a wave of the hand, Sir Arthur knocked over a glass of water, spilling it over the gentlemen of the press.

"So sorry"! he said, his eyes twinkling, "I seem to have baptised you, even if I don't succeed in converting you."

☆

11. Two ardent Republicans were having their child christened, before the war. In the church the father was holding the baby in front of the baptismal font. When asked the

Christian name of the child, he gave the name of Roosevelt.

His wife, an anti-Roosevelt, looked askant. After the ceremony she said "Why in the name of God did you call him after that name? You know how I dislike the sound of his name."

"Well," replied the husband, "I just couldn't resist it. As I held our child in our arms, he started smiling at me. And in a little while he was soaking me."

☆

12. Two Jews named Levy and Lamech went together to the baptismal font, and the first to be called for baptism was Levy. When he came out of the font after baptism, Lamech greeted him eagerly, "Well, Levy, how did it go?" Levy paid scant attention to his friend and started to move away.

"I say," said Lamech, "what's the matter with you?"

"Nothing is the matter with me," said Levy, sharply. "In the first place, my name is not Levy, it's Mathew. In the second place, I don't have anything to say to you Jews. You crucified our Lord!"

☆

13. An old mountaineer late in a sinful life, was being baptised. Mother and the kids sat with the crowd on the creek bank. As the preacher led the man out belt-deep in the water, there before God and everybody, the ace and king of Spades were seen to float out of the man's pocket. Then came the queen and the jack and just as the preacher was ready to souse the man under, came the ten of Spades. Old wife jumped up, "Preacher, Preacher," she yelled, "don't baptise him. He is lost!"

But the oldest boy jumped up and yelled: "No, he ain't, mother. Go ahead preacher. If dad can't win with that hand, he can't make it at all."

☆

14. Menachem Lefkowitz was baptised in the Calvary Lutheran Church. He rose from the altar and the preacher shook his hand. "Now that you have been baptised, you may choose a Christian name if you wish," he said. "Have you thought of any name?"

23

"Yes, Reverend, I have," answered Lefkowitz. "I would like to be called Martin Luther."

"That's fine," beamed the preacher, "you certainly have chosen an historic Christian name. May I know the reason?"

"It's like this, Reverend," explained ex-Menachem Lefkowitz, "I don't want to change the initials on my Laundry."

☆

15. One preacher was baptising an elderly woman who was deathly frightened about going beneath the water. The woman struggled as the preacher tried to put her under. The whole time she clung to the side of the baptistry with her right hand.

After the service, the preacher met the woman in the vestibule, commenting, "Dear Lady, if I believed in baptismal regeneration, I would have to consign your right hand to perdition."

☆

16. A young Jewish man called on a priest and expressed his desire to join the Catholic Church. The priest was elated and said, "My son, I am indeed happy that you have come to know the greatness of Christianity. Today I am a bit busy. Could you see me a couple of days later so that I may instruct you on our true and great faith?"

"But that will be too late, Father," insisted the young man. "I want to get baptised right now and here."

"Why the hurry? A great religion like ours cannot be imparted in a few minutes."

"Well, it's like this, Father," explained the young Jew, "I just had a terrible fight with my wife and before I cool off, I want to do something immediately to disgrace her."

5
THE BIBLE

1. A Bible in the hand is worth two in the bookcase.

☆

2. Dust on the Bible is not evidence that it is a dry book.

☆

3. The Bible contains the vitamins for a healthy soul.

☆

4. Bible verses will save you from spiritual reverses.

☆

5. Read your Bible. A chapter a day keeps Satan away.

☆

6. Satan is not afraid of a Bible with dust on it.

☆

7. Other books were given to us for information, but the Bible was given to us for transformation.

☆

8. If all the neglected Bibles in this country were dusted off at the same time, we would suffer the worst dust storm in years.

☆

9. An immoral man is dangerous whether he is armed with a rifle or a Bible.

☆

10. The three greatest sins of today are, indifference to, neglect of and disrespect for the Word of God.

☆

11. Sir Dingle Foot, the distinguished lawyer politician, once admitted that he had inadvertently given Her Majesty's judges a lecture on their sex lives. Former legal adviser to the

Wilson Government, Sir Dingle read the Bible lesson to a congregation of judges and attorneys and their wives at a service in Gray's Inn, in London. He should have read from the first chapter of St. Paul's First Epistle to Corinthians. By mistake he read from the Fifth chapter and it went like this:-

"I actually hear reports of sexual immorality among you, immorality such as pagans do not tolerate."

The judges squirmed. So did their wives.

Sir Dingle ploughed on: "Your satisfaction ill becomes you." On to the last verse: "You are judges within the fellowship. Root out the evil doer within your community."

Sir Dingle told newsmen he quickly realised he was on the wrong track when he saw the parson raise his eyes in surprise and supplication. "But by then it was too late," he said.

☆

12. A Washington religious bookshop in order to attract customers put this bit of versification on a card in the window:-

Holy Scripture, Writ Divine,
At a dollar fortynine;
Satan trembles when he sees,
Bibles sold as cheap as these.

☆

13. While campaigning in an election, the minister for housing was having a hard time in explaining his government's scanty performance in regard to housing programme to his constituents. A clergyman, who was sitting by the minister on the podium, got up, and remarked in a reassuring tone, "Don't feel too small, Sir, as a voter and a student of the Bible, I am convinced that your government is doing pretty well. In fact, I believe your government is following the good Biblical example. For in, First Kings, Chapter 9, Verse 10, we find, 'And it came to pass at the end of twenty years, when Solomon had built two houses...'"

☆

14. A parson of a stately appearance was once asked why he wore a belt and suspender. Eyes sparkling, he replied that

26

he was faithfully emulating the good Biblical advice, and quoted Ecclesiastes IV: 9-10:- "Two are better than one because they have a good reward for their labour. For if they fall, the one will lift up his fellow; but woe to him that is alone when he falleth; for he hath not another to help him up."

☆

15. An old minister grew tall in the estimation of his female parishioners because he always made it his happy business to keep them in good humour. To further endear himself to them, one Sunday morning he said, "If your husband refuses to wipe dishes, claiming that it is not a man's job, reach for the Holy Bible and read from the Second Kings, 21:13- "And I will wipe Jerusalem as a man wipeth a dish, wiping it, and turning it upside down'."

The female parishioners smiled while the men sqirmed in their seats.

☆

16. When the government was enrolling recruits for compulsory service in the armed forces a newly wed used a Bible quotation to be excused from army duty: "When a man hath taken a new wife, he shall not go out to war, neither shall he be charged with any business, but he shall be free at home one year, and shall cheer up his wife which he hath taken." (Deuteronomy 24:5). The recruiting officer sent him home.

☆

17. A RHYME FOR REMEMBERING THE OLD TESTAMENT

The great Jehovah speaks to us,
In Genesis and Exodus,
Leviticus and Numbers see,
Followed by Deuteronomy.
Joshua and Judges sway the land,
Ruth gleans a sheaf with trembling hand.
Samuel and numerous Kings appear,
Whose Chronicles we wondering hear;
Ezra and Nehemiah now,
Esther the beauteous mourner show;
Job speaks in sighs, David in Psalms,

27

The Proverbs teach to scatter alms.
Ecclesiastes then comes on,
And the sweet Song of Solomon.
Isaiah, Jeremiah then,
With Lamentations takes his pen,
Ezekiel, Daniel, Hosea's lyres,
Swell Joel, Amos, Obadaiah's
Next Jonah, Micah, Nahum come,
And lofty Habakkuk finds room.
Rapt Zephaniah, Haggai calls,
While Zechariah builds the walls.
And Malachi, with garments rent,
Concludes the ancient Testament.

☆

18. An American makes a proposal to the Vatican; he offers a hundred million dollars in exchange for the changing of one word in the Bible. He will only reveal what the word is when meeting with the Pope himself. The Curia is doubtful, but the money would be useful. An audience is arranged, but it does not last long.

"What did you propose?" the puzzled cardinals ask the American.

"Only that 'Amen' should be replaced by Texas Oil".

☆

19. In the days when the late Colonel Edward H. R. Green, railroad industrialist and Banker, was managing the Texas Midland Railroad for his mother, the astute Hetty Green — known to fame as "The richest woman in America" — he was having a lot of trouble with applicants for passes over the line, and so consulted his mother about it. She mentioned the matter to her friend Chauncey M. Depew, who knew all about railroads, being a high official of the New York Central. Depew gave her a list of Biblical quotations, which she forwarded to her son.

The list was arranged as a calendar in this manner:-

Monday   — "Thou shalt not pass..."   (Num. 20:18)
Tuesday   — "Suffer not a man to pass..." (Judg. 3:28)
Wednesday   — "The wicked shall no more pass"

(Nah. 1:15)

28

Thursday	— "This generation shall not pass..."
	(Mark 13:30)
Friday	— "By a perpetual decree it cannot pass..."
	(Jer. 5:22)
Saturday	— "None shall pass..." (Isa. 34:10)
Sunday	— "So he paid the fare thereof and went..."
	(Jonah 1:3)

☆

20. John D. Rockefeller Jr once asked a clergyman to give him an appropriate Bible verse on which to base an address he was to make at the latter's church.

"I was thinking," said Rockefeller, "that I would take the verse from the Twenty-Third Psalm: 'The Lord is my shepherd.' Would that seem appropriate?"

"Quite," said the clergyman. "But do you really want an appropriate verse?

"I certainly do," was the reply.

"Well, then," said the clergyman, with a twinkle in his eye, "I would select the verse in the same psalm: 'Thou anointest my head with oil; my cup runneth over'."

☆

21. Abraham Lincoln was an intelligent judge of art. At a friend's house he was once shown a picture done by an amateur and was asked his opinion of it. "I can truthfully say," said Abe, "that the painter has observed the Commandments."

"How so?" asked the owner of the painting.

"Because," said Lincoln, "he hath not made to himself the likeness of anything in heaven above, or that which is on earth beneath, or that which is in the water under the earth."

☆

22. Mrs Cornelius Vanderbilt had her servant troubles, too. Once she obtained what she thought was the perfect parlour maid. Then one day the maid gave notice without warning. She had seemed to like the work and no one could understand why she had decided to leave.

When told of the woman's decision, Mrs Vanderbilt sent for her. "Why do you wish to leave, Florence?" she asked, with a pained expression on her face. "Is anything wrong?"

29

3

"Yes," answered Florence. "I just can't stand the suspense in this house."

"Suspense? What do you mean?"

"You see, Madame," the maid continued respectfully, "Over my bed is a sign which says; 'Watch ye. For ye know not when the master cometh'."

6
CARDINAL WIT

1. Cardinal Saint Robert Bellarmine, who carefully guarded his sight, went once to visit a prince, and in the lobby where he had to wait for some time, he saw some very obscene pictures that made him sick. He never said anything about it to the prince during the audience, but on saying goodbye he remarked, "I would like to recommend to your Highness some poor people who do not have necessary clothes to cover their nakedness."

"I shall be very glad to perform this charitable act," replied the prince, walking the Cardinal to the door. When they reached the lobby the Cardinal, pointing to the pictures, said, "These are the naked people I spoke to you about."

The prince understood, and had the pictures taken down immediately.

☆

2. The following episode took place between Napoleon and Cardinal Consalvi. Napoleon was annoyed because every time the Cardinal was able to see Pope Pius VII, he systematically undid everything the Emperor had obtained from the Pontiff. Now Napoleon faced his enemy and very angrily shouted, "I want you to know that I can destroy the Pope and your Church."

"Your Majesty," smiled the Cardinal, "even *we* have not succeeded in doing this for the past eighteen centuries."

☆

3. Cardinal Hinsley was once called upon to give evidence in a court case, and to impress the jury, the defence counsel asked if he was the leader of the English Catholics.

"That's right," said the Cardinal.

"In fact you are the Prince of the Church of Rome?"

"Correct."

"One of the greatest scholars not only in England but also in the world?"

"True."

"A brilliant man in every way?"

"Yes."

Later a friend reproached the Cardinal, "You weren't very humble today. Were you?"

The Cardinal smiled, "True," he said, "but what could I do? I was on oath."

☆

4. The late Cardinal Hinsley of Great Britain and the Archbishop of Canterbury attended the same dinner party and later shared a taxicab into the town. "It's quite fitting that we take the same cab together," smiled the archbishop. "After all we both serve God."

"Yes, yes," agreed the Cardinal heartily, "you in your way, I in His."

Cardinal Hinsley liked to tell the story of two brothers who studied for ministry. One was a little flippant and whimsical to reach the heights, the other a pompous and heavy-handed party, became a bishop in due course. "My brother," the whimsical one explained, "rose because of his gravity, I was held down by levity."

☆

5. New York's Cardinal Spellman was watching a World Series baseball game, back in the days when they had such things in Brooklyn, and a high foul fly was hit toward his box seat. Roy Campanella, the catcher, tried to reach it but missed and the ball bounced against the Cardinal's knee. Roy enquired anxiously if he had been hurt.

"Don't worry about it, Roy," the Cardinal said, "A priest's knees are the toughest and the most thickly padded part of his anatomy."

☆

6. Cardinal Francis Spellman relates this personal experience. "During my recent trip overseas, Cardinal Machory invited all the bishops of Northern Ireland to meet me. He had been fortunate enough to secure a large fish for dinner and it reminded me of one I had seen mounted in a friend's office in the States.

"When some newspapers asked me a great many questions which no human being could possibly answer, I pointed
to the fish on the platter and told them of the mounted fish
back home with the significant label: If I had kept my mouth
shut, I wouldn't be here."

☆

7. Cardinal Manning, the English churchman, was the
author of a book called, "CONFIDENCE IN GOD." One day,
requiring a copy for his own use, he called at a book shop for
it.

The clerk called downstairs to the keeper of the store-
room, "One copy of Manning's 'Confidence in God'."

In a few moments the answer came up the stairs,
"Manning's 'CONFIDENCE IN GOD' all gone."

☆

8. Cardinal Manning was so severe a teetotaller that he
sternly reminded an Irish priest that twenty five per cent of
the criminals are drinkers.

To this the simple priest replied, "Indeed, Your Eminence,
and I never knew that the teetotallers had so high a percent-
age."

☆

9. Sir John Green Borough's contribution is about a
bachelor posted as ambassador to Peru. At a reception dance
given by him in the embassy he spent more time with his
whiskey bottle than with his guests. Emboldened by the
intake of spirits he decided to ask what appeared to him his
most important lady guest, to dance a Viennese Waltz with
him. The guest turned down the request with the following
words: "There are three reasons why I will not dance with you.
The first is that you have obviously had too much to drink.
The second is that the orchestra is not playing a Viennese
Waltz, it is playing the Peruvian national anthem. And
thirdly, I am the Cardinal Bishop of Buenos Aires."

☆

10. He (Cardinal John Henry Newman) was travelling in
a railway carriage and sitting opposite were a couple of men

who made continual and derogatory remarks about the Church. The Cardinal said not a word until one of the men came to his destination. As the man was getting out of the train, the Cardinal said, "Here. You've forgotten something behind."

The man turned round quickly. "Have I left something behind?"

"Yes," said the Cardinal, "a very bad impression."

☆

11. Cardinal Manning once attended a dinner at which he sat next to Dr Alder, the Chief Rabbi, when a huge ham was passed round. Cardinal Manning turned to the Rabbi and asked, "Dr Alder, when are you going to be liberal enough to eat ham?"

The Chief Rabbi smiled and said, "At your Eminence's wedding."

☆

12. Of his first days at Boston College High School, Cardinal Cushing tells of this story on himself: "We had to serve Mass in rotation and eventually my turn came. Well, I had never served in my life, but I thought I did pretty well. At the end of the Mass, while the priest was taking off his vestments, he made a practice of telling each of us what mistakes we had made. By way of criticizing how I had served he said, 'I am not going to ask you if you have served a Mass, before have you ever *seen* one?"

☆

13. A lady with more naivette than good sense, approached Cardinal Gibbon and asked, "Your Eminence, with all your ability and brilliance, surely you can't believe in papal infallibility."

"Well," said the Cardinal, "the last time when I was in Rome, the Holy Father called me Jibbons."

☆

14. Monsignor Arthur J. Scanlan of St Helena's Church in the Bronx, New York always omitted his title whenever he

34

referred to himself. One night he answered the phone with his usual, "Hello. This is Father Scanlan speaking."

There was a pause at the other end, then a chuckle from the Cardinal's residence "Well," the voice said, "this is Father Spellman."

☆

15. Cardinal Wyzynski, the Primate of Poland, while on his way to Rome stopped at Venice, because the train would halt there for 45 minutes. Cardinal Angelo Giuseppe Roncalli invited him for a boat trip on the Grand Canal. The Primate of Poland enjoyed the boat trip to his heart's content. But soon he glanced at his watch and cried, "My God, my train has left!"

Eyes twinkling, Roncalli said, "Don't worry, Your Eminence. That gentleman in the motorboat is the station-master. I have kidnapped him. The train would not budge an inch without him."

☆

16. When Cardinal Roncalli (the future Pope John XXIII) met famous Catholic literateur Father Daniel Rops, for the first time, he said to him with an affected sigh: "Ah, Father, we must together pray to the Lord to take away half the extra fat from me and present it to you!"

☆

17. During World War II, Francis Cardinal Spellman often used to spend his Christmas overseas with the armed forces. On one visit, a colonel was showing the Cardinal the maps and photographs of some recent action, when through an interoffice speaker came a voice saying, "There's a little fellow in a clergyman's collar over to see you. Give him the two-dollar show."

The colonel informed the voice that the distinguished guest was already there and so the speaker suddenly clicked off. Though highly embarrassed, the colonel showed Cardinal Spellman the works. While leaving the place, His Eminence thanked the colonel and others and with eyes gleaming said, "I thought that show was worth at least three dollars."

35

7
CATHOLICS AND PROTESTANTS

1. Pat and Bridget had seventeen children so the Vatican decided to present them with a gold medal specially struck in their honour. The Papal Nuncio delivered the medal in person and told them they were a credit to the Catholic Church.

"There must be some mistake," said Pat. "We're Protestants."

"Oh, my God," said the Papal Nuncio, "don't tell me we've minted a gold medal for two sex-crazy Protestants."

☆

2. HOLY SMOKE

> I am the Vicar of St Paul's
> And I'm ringing the steeple bell,
> The floor of the church is on fire,
> or the lid has come off hell.
>
> Shall I ring the fire brigade?
> Or should I trust in the Lord?
> Oh, dear; I've just remembered
> I don't think we've insured.
>
> "What's this then?" said the fire chief,
> "Is this church C of E?
> It is? Then we can't put it out
> My lads are all R.C."

☆

3. Two road workers, Protestant and Catholic, were making repairs when a Catholic priest passed by and entered a saloon. "Isn't that a shame?" observed the Protestant worker. "A man of cloth has no business in a saloon. He should be visiting the sick."

Just then a protestant minister entered the same saloon.

The same workman now remarked, "There must be somebody pretty sick there."

☆

4. A little Protestant boy in East Belfast was standing in the street, crying his eyes out. A lady stopped to console him.

"What's the matter, little boy?"

Between sobs the boy replied, "My father doesn't love me."

"Of course he does," she tried to reassure him, "what makes you say such a thing?"

"He's been back to vote three times since he died, but he's never come to see me once."

☆

5. An Irish Protestant who was dangerously ill and believed he was dying sent for a Catholic priest and was received into the Roman Church. His Protestant friends were horrified and one of them asked him how he could thus forsake the creed for which he had stood all his life and go over to the enemy."

"Well," said the sick man, "It is this way. I said to myself, if any one's got to die better one of their lot than one of our lot."

☆

6. Bob Consdine told the story of a Notre Dame star who went to a sterling but absent-minded priest every week for confession. The priest had the habit of marking the number of sins on his sleeve with a piece of chalk in order to mete out the proper penance.

"Father," said the player one day, "I ran clear across the field to chip a player in our last game."

"That was very wrong, my son," said the priest, making a chalk mark.

"When he fell, I kicked him in the teeth."

"How terrible, son! Will you never learn true Christianity?" (four more marks) "And when the referee was not looking, I chewed off a piece of his ear."

"Saints save us! You're a disgrace to your teachers and college." By this time the chalk marks were clear up to the

37

priest's elbow.

"What was the team you were playing, my son?"

"Southern Methodists," said the player.

"Oh," beamed the priest, rubbing off every mark on his sleeve. "I guess, boys will be boys!"

☆

7. A conservative lady in Belfast would take a cart from the station only if it were driven by a Protestant. The driver, who was not a church-goer, said, "I admit I have not been into a church for the last twenty years — I assure you that my horse is a Protestant."

"What makes you say that your horse is a Protestant?"

"Madam, I have had him twenty years and never once have I seen him on his knees."

☆

8. A priest ran out of gasoline about six blocks from a filling station, and he walked there for a can of gasoline. The filling station manager was embarrassed because he didn't have a gasoline can. "The people have walked off with cans in the past week," he said. "But, we'll figure out something."

He did. He came up with the idea of filling a dozen empty cold drinks cans with gasoline and putting them in two six pack cartons. With one six pack in each hand the priest walked back to his car and proceeded to pour the gasoline into the tank.

Just at that time, a Methodist minister, who was a friend of his, drove by. When he recognized his friend, he backed up to see if he could be of help. As he watched the priest empty the cold drinks cans into his tank, he said, "I must admit one thing. You Catholics sure do have more faith than we Methodists."

☆

9. Walking down the street, two hillbillies met a Catholic nun whose arm was in a sling.

"What's wrong with your arm, Sister?" asked one hillbilly.

"It's broken in three places," the Sister replied.

"How did that happen?" asked the second hillbilly.

"I slipped in the bathtub," answered the Sister.

After leaving, the first hillbilly asked the other, "What is a bathtub?"

"Heck, I don't know," said his friend, "I'm not Catholic."

☆

10. Two Catholics met in a pub in Dublin.

"Sure, Mike, I've been working in London doing the best job in the world."

"And what might that be?"

"I work in a crematorium."

"Oh! My God! You don't call that a good job, do you?"

"Sure, it is," replied Larry, "what could be better than burning Protestants and getting paid for it too!"

☆

11. A minister, driving at 80 miles per hour, was very much piqued to notice a motorcycle policeman trying to overtake him. The minister drew up at the side of the road and the policeman stopped beside him. "Why didn't you stop when I hollered at your back there?" asked the policeman with anger writ large on his face.

"Oh," said the clever minister, "I suppose I heard you say, 'Good afternoon, Father'."

"That I did, Father," smiled the officer, "But I wanted to warn you about the next township — there's a damned Protestant on duty there."

☆

12. It was a game between the rough playing team of Notre Dame and the University of Pennsylvania. It was a keenly contested match. The former team always prayed before the start of the game, and were hell bent upon winning the match. After a very rough play, the captain of Pennsylvania team called time and sought out the referee.

"Sir, I want to protest the deliberate roughness of Notre Dame. Their big centre bites my leg everytime he gets the chance in a pile-up. What can be done about his taking a bite out of me?"

The referee said with a smile, "I would suggest rescheduling to play them only on Friday."

☆

13. An Irish Catholic policeman who was a little drunk
went into a church, where he fell asleep. The sexton woke him
up and told him that he was closing up.

"What do you mean?" said the constable. "The cathedral
never closes."

"This is not the cathedral," said the sexton. "This is a
Presbyterian church."

The Irish cop looked around him. On the walls were
paintings of the apostles. "Isn't that Saint Luke over there?"
he inquired.

"Yes, you are right," said the sexton.

"And Saint Mark just beyond him?"

"Yes."

"Tell me," said the cop, "since when did they all become
Presbyterians?"

8
CHRISTIANS AND JEWS

1. While on his parish rounds Father O'Brien sees three children playing together—two small strangers and Michael O'Conner, one of his flock. He stops, is introduced and, thinking of priestly duties, tells the children he'll give £2 to whoever can answer the question "who was the greatest man on earth?"

The boys think for a minute and one of the strangers, Mark Bunyan, bursts out, "President Kennedy."

"Sure, now," says the priest, "he was a good man all right, but not the greatest. Come now, Michael," he prompts, "you should know this if you remember your catechism."

"Well, Father," says Michael, "I'd say it was St Patrick because he brought Christianity to England."

"No Michael. It's a good answer, but not the right one," says the priest, and he confidently pockets the £2.

But Isaac Goldstein, the other stranger, pipes up: "It was Jesus Christ."

The priest pays up, but with a puzzled air. "Isaac," he asks, "surely someone of your faith doesn't believe that?"

"Oh no, Father, I know Moses was the greatest. But business is business."

☆

2. A Rabbi had the misfortune to run his car into the side of Father Murphy's car. He jumped out straight away and ran to Father Murphy who was still sitting in the driver's seat, looking pale.

The Rabbi was loud with apologies. "My dear Father Murphy, how sorry I am that I should be so silly as to do this to you of all people, a fellow man of God! Are you all right?"

"Oh, yes, no injuries, Rabbi," said the priest, "but I am a bit shaken."

"Oh course, you are," said the Rabbi with great concern. "Here have a sip of this; it's good whisky!" And he handed a hip flask to the priest who thanked him and drank heartily.

"Go on, Father Murphy, have another! It's all my fault. Drink deep! Don't worry about the cost."

Father Murphy needed no second bidding and took another deep swing. "Won't you have one, Rabbi?"

"With the police arriving already?"

☆

3. A Catholic, a Protestant and a Jew were on the ill-fated TITANIC when she struck the iceberg. As she started to sink, a voice shouted: "We're going to meet our Maker — we'd better do something religious!"

So the Catholic said a prayer, the Protestant sang, "Bread of Heaven," — and the Jew took a collection.

☆

4. George Jessel gets the credit for the story about the devout Catholic girl who fell desperately in love with a Jewish lad. "Teach him the Virtues of Catholicism," counselled her mother. "Make a convert of him!" "That's just what I will do," promised the girl and she set to work with a will that very evening.

The Jewish lad proved an easy convert. He waxed more and more enthusiastic as the days went by. Suddenly, however, one day before the wedding, the bridegroom called all bets off. "What happened?" cried the distracted mother.

"I oversold him," wept the girl. "He wants to be a priest!"

☆

5. The distraught young man was perched on the 40th floor ledge of a skyscraper in New York and threatened to jump. The closest the police could get was the roof of an adjacent building, a few feet below. However, all pleas to the man to return to safety were of no avail. A Catholic priest was summoned and he hastened to the scene.

"Think, my son," he intoned to the would be suicide, "think of your mother and father who love you."

"Ah, they don't love me. I am jumping."

"No, stop," cried the priest, "think of the woman who loves you."

"Nobody loves me. I am jumping."

42

"But think," implored the priest, "think of Holy Mary, who loves you."

"Holy Mary!" queried the man, "who is she?"

At which point the cleric yelled back, "Jump, you Jew bastard, jump!"

☆

6. A Rabbi, who sat by the driver (a priest) in a Volkswagon, saw to his great horror, a truck coming at them at a very high speed. The Rabbi quickly made a sign of the cross, just as the priest pulled the car to the right and avoided the most gruesome accident.

"Say, Rabbi," said the priest, "I noticed you crossed yourself at that frightening moment. Did you forget that you were a Rabbi?"

"What forget?" he answered, "who had time to make a Star of David?"

☆

7. A priest went into a tailor's shop and placed an order for a new suit. When he asked how much it would cost, the tailor replied, "I hold the clergy in high regard and never charge them." So the next day the priest sent the tailor a nice crucifix.

Then a Rabbi went into the shop and ordered a new suit. When asked what the stitching charges were, the tailor replied that he never charged the Rabbis. So the next day the Rabbi sent three more Rabbis.

☆

8. I told this story the other night to several thousand Republican ladies about how Mr Kruschev had certain problems. He found that Stalin's body haunted him and finally he figured the best way to fix that was to get rid of Stalin's body. So he called President Kennedy and asked if he'd take the body. Kennedy explained he didn't want a communist dead or alive in the United States, but suggested he call MacMillan. MacMillan gave Kruschev the same line, that he would like to help him but it would cause too much political trouble and suggested: "Try De Gaulle. Every once in a while that fellow will help you and besides he enjoys offending Americans."

Well, De Gaulle explained to Kruschev that he had trouble at home and abroad but suggested he try Ben-Gurion. "There's a little fellow who's pretty decent, and his country has the most relaxed immigration laws. He'll probably help you." So Kruschev called Ben-Gurion, told him his dilemma, and said, "We'll bring the body in the dark of night and absolutely clandestinely and you won't have anything to worry about." Ben-Gurion answered "Oh, Mr Kruschev, don't give it a thought. We're tickled to death to help you. Just bring that body in broad day light. We'll take care of it. But I have to remind you, Mr Kruschev, that my country has the highest rate of Resurrection in the world." — Senator Goldwater.

☆

9. In the Bronx, Helen Goldblatt saw a throng lining the Grand Concourse to cheer Cardinal Spellman. Loudest of the cheerers was a little old Jewish lady holding her grand-daughter aloft to catch a glimpse of the passing prelate. "It's very nice of you to get excited over Cardinal Spellman," observed Miss Goldblatt.

"Cardinal Spellman?" echoed the startled lady. "I thought it was Mischa Elman!"

☆

10. Three clergymen, a Rabbi, a Protestant minister and a Catholic priest were arrested for playing three-handed cards for a small stake in a blue-law town, one night. Immediately they were produced before a Lay Magistrate, who after listening to the charge against them, grimly asked the priest, "Were you gambling, Father?"

The priest looked heavenward and after asking God's forgiveness, said aloud to the Magistrate, "No, Your Honour, I was not gambling."

"Were you gambling, Reverend?" the Lay Magistrate asked the Protestant minister, who like the Catholic priest, looked heavenward for forgiveness before he answered the L.M., "No, Your Honour, I was not gambling."

Then the L.M. addressed the third clergyman, "Were you gambling, Rabbi?"

Looking at the Magistrate with an air of indifference, the Rabbi replied, "With whom?"

11. A Rabbi and a priest were discussing the achievements of Judaism and Christianity. "Rabbi, without meaning any disparagement to your men of science," said the priest, "we Catholics were the first modern scientists."

"What makes you think so?" asked the Rabbi.

"Well, only a few years ago, while digging the catacombs where the early Christians hid from the Romans, a group of archeologists uncovered a long wire."

"What does that signify?"

"It proves that we Catholics were the inventors of telegraphy, almost two thousand years ago."

"Frankly," said the Rabbi, "I don't see anything surprising about that. When the archeologists dug out the Dead Sea Scrolls, did you know they dug a hole thirty feet deep and there on the bottom, was no wire at all."

"What in the world does that prove?"

"That proves that long before the Christian Era, we Jews had wireless!"

9
CHUCKLES IN THE VATICAN

1. Pope John XXIII served with an Italian medical unit as a non-commissioned officer during the 1st World War. At an audience for Italian bishops, Pope John caught sight of Bishop Arrigo Pintonello, chief chaplain of the Italian army, wearing a General's uniform.

As Bishop Pintonello prepared to genuflect and kiss the papal ring, the Pope stepped forward smiling, and saluted. "Sir," he said, "Sergeant Roncalli, at your command."

☆

2. When Pope John XXIII was asked how many people worked in the Vatican, he replied with a smile, "About half of them."

☆

3. A Cardinal asked Paul III for a favour but since what he wanted was not very fair, the Pope made it difficult to obtain, and the Cardinal said, "Your Holiness knows very well how hard I worked to make you Pope, and therefore, you should not deny me this favour."

The Supreme Pontiff replied, "Since you made me a Pope, let me be one."

☆

4. One day Leo XII went to visit a convent church which he had been told was very much neglected. He entered the church without being seen and knelt down in a pew, and then went to the convent and spoke very affably to all. When leaving, the father superior begged him, "Holy Father, do you wish to leave us a remembrance of the high honour you have bestowed on us?"

"A remembrance?" said the Pope smiling. "Go to the church and look at the pew in which I was kneeling and you will find a remembrance there."

As soon as the Pope left, everybody went to the church to see the 'remembrance' and on the layer of dust covering the pew they saw this name written in large letters: "LEO XII".

☆

5. When in 1804 Napoleon proposed with pleasant words to Pius VII his unworthy plans for the Church, the Pope simply replied: "Comedian."

"What," exclaimed the Emperor, "me a comedian? This is the end of everything." He furiously picked up from the table an artistic mosaic depicting St Peter's Basilica and throwing it at the Pontiff's feet, he shouted, "Look, old man, I will crush your kingdom just like that."

The Pope got up just as impressively as he had entered and left the room saying only one word, "Tragedian."

And Napoleon's fate was a tragedy from then on. The old man still was living when Napoleon died on Saint Helena.

☆

6. An artist asked for and received permission to draw a portrait of the Pope. After the Portrait had been completed he asked for the Pope's autograph.

The Pope scrutinised the likeness of himself very carefully and then wrote "Verily it is as though ye know me not!"

☆

7. On the occasion of an audience granted by the Pope, a French doctor said to the Pontifical Sovereign: "Holy Father, among the French doctors there are a great number of Roman Catholic practitioners. Those ask you to bless their works."

Pius XI answered, "I do not only bless your works, your houses, your families, but above all, I bless your patients."

☆

8. Pope Pius IX was a man with keen sense of humour, and many good stories testify to it. He was known for the informality of his audiences when he would engage members in conversation and occasionally cause a ripple of laughter with his humour. Once he spoke to a very fat English-woman.

"What brings you to Rome?" asked His Holiness.

"Faith, Your Holiness! Faith!"

47

"Well," replied the Pope, "they say that faith can move mountains, so you have come to the right place."

☆

9. Another time an American woman said to him: "I must tell Your Holiness that I paid five hundred dollars for a pair of your old socks to cure my arthritis."

"And did they help you?"

"Oh, yes indeed," said the pilgrim, "I never had arthritis again in my life."

"Interesting," replied the Pope. "I can assure you that they never helped me. My arthritis is as bad as ever."

☆

10. It seems incredible that an American gangster was received in audience by a Pope but it is a fact that the notorious 'Bugsie' Siegal was not only received at the Vatican, but was also decorated by the Pope.

It all began with a certain Contessa de Frasso, an American leader of Cafe Society, who first introduced 'Bugsie' to Prince Umberto, who in turn arranged an audience with his father, the King of Italy. It followed as a matter of course that the Pope would also receive anyone as distinguished as 'Bugsie' seemed to be.

And so the audience with 'Bugsie' was arranged, during which a minor decoration was pinned on the gangster. After the brief ceremony, a Vatican official had the (rather late) good sense to look up 'Bugsie' Siegal in the dossiers and to his horror he found that this man who had been honoured by His Holiness was not the sort of person who ought to receive anything, let alone an audience or a minor decoration from a Pope of Rome.

Something had to be done immediately. Orders were given a Papal messenger to go to 'Bugsie' Siegal's hotel and demand the decoration from him. The emissary arrived just in time to find 'Bugsie' preening himself in the mirror at his hotel suite.

"What do you want?" he asked sharply, annoyed at being disturbed.

"I am sorry, Mr Siegal," said the emissary, "I must ask

48

you for the return of the medal. There has been an error..."

"And whose error?" demanded "Bugsie" discourteously.

Meekly, almost apologetically, the man murmured, "It was an error of His Holiness."

"Bugsie" took another look at himself in the mirror, then turned sharply to the emissary, "It is impossible for the Pope to make an error. He is infallible."

He kept the medal.

11. Pope Leo XII in 1825, visited a jail. His Holiness called the prisoners before him and asked each prisoner why he had been jailed. In each case the criminal protested innocence; all except one. "Your Holiness," said the wild-looking fellow falling on his feet, "I was a forger and an assassin and I am here to expiate my crimes."

The Pope turned to his entourage with an ironic smile, and said to the governor of the prison, "Let this rascal go at once; I do not wish that his presence should corrupt all these gallant and innocent gentlemen."

12. When Giacoma Cardinal Della Chiesa, Archbishop of Bologna, was elected as Pope Benedict XV, 1914, the first thing he did was to go through the unattended documents left by his predecessor on the papal writing desk. Among them, he found a confidential report from the bishop of Cologne warning the Supreme Pontiff about the radical views of his superior, Cardinal Della Chiesa and the danger he represents to the church.

Pope Benedict wrote in Latin across the report: "Almighty has decided differently." He signed it and sent it back to the hapless bishop much to his discomfiture.

13. Once a Cardinal who was seriously ill sent a messenger to Pope Pius IX asking his special blessings. "I send you my blessing most willingly." said the Pope, "but I also recommend that you take some quinine."

14. An American was getting a haircut preparatory to a trip to Europe. "Where are you going?" asked the barber. "Oh, to London, to Paris, and then to Rome," answered his customer. "You won't like it," muttered the barber. "London is foggy. Paris is too crowded and hectic. And Rome — why it seems the whole world is going there. I guess you think you'll see the Pope. Man, you can't get anywhere near him." When the American returned and sat down for another haircut, the barber asked. "How was the trip?" "Swell," said the American. "It was sunny and bright in London. Paris was very enjoyable. And when I got to Rome, I had a personal audience with the Holy Father. He even blessed me and spoke to me." "What did he say?", the barber eagerly asked. "Well, I knelt down for his blessing, and when he put his hands on my head, he said, "Where the devil did you get that haircut?"

☆

15. A few minutes before receiving Jacqueline Kennedy, Pope John XXIII asked Cardinal Cicognani how he had to address the First Lady. The latter said, "Holy Father, you may address her as 'Madam or Mrs President."

But the minute Mrs Kennedy crossed the threshold, the Supreme Pontiff rushed forward with open arms and cried in excitement, "Hello, Jacqueline!"

☆

16. American ambassador to Vatican, Robert Murphy met Pope Pius XII in 1944 after the Allies had entered Rome. Murphy reminded the Supreme Pontiff that he had first met him as a junior foreign-service officer in Berlin in 1931, when Eugene Pacelli was Vatican Secretary of State. Murphy recalled the papal secretary's prediction that the newly-installed Chancellor, Adolph Hitler was only a passing phase.

"Ah," replied the Holy Father, "but that was before I was infallible."

☆

17. Golda Meir, was on a visit in Rome to see Pope Paul. Being Jew, she was a bit nervous of visiting the Supreme Pontiff of the Catholic Church. In all humility she said to an

aide in the Vatican, "Just imagine, Golda Meir, daughter of a poor American carpenter, going in to talk with the head of Rome."

"Mind your language," said the papal aide, "carpentry is considered a very esteemed profession around here."

☆

18. Three braggarts — a Virginian, a Californian and a Texan became friends during their stay at a resort in Switzerland. One fine afternoon, while they were sipping tea together in a restaurant, the Virginian said, "Talking about the Middle East, I told George..."

"President George Bush?" asked the Californian.

"That's right. This was just two months ago. I had lunch with him and he asked me to stay for dinner also, and we talked about the Middle East. Unfortunately, he didn't pay heed to my sage advice."

Not to be outdone by the Virginian, the Californian said, "I wonder if what you had to say was anything like what Maggie told me."

"Maggie?" said the Virginian.

"I mean, Margaret Thatcher, the Iron Lady of United Kingdom. We have known each other since her college days. I spent a weekend with her family last month. She holds me in high esteem. Now what she said about the Middle East..."

But now the Texan interrupted, "When I was in Rome with John Paul, last month..."

"John Paul who?" chorused the other two.

"His Holiness, John Paul, the Pope," said the Texan calmly. "He is a friend of mine. He is a Catholic and I am a Protestant, but friends are friends. I was with him on a big holiday during the course of which he was carried on a big throne through the streets of Rome on the shoulders of a dozen people. Since he was feeling lonely, he pleaded with me to sit by his side on the throne. Of course, I obliged him as a favour to a good friend. From the throne I could see a concourse of people jostling and whispering, "who is that handsome man sitting by the side of the Texan?"

10
CHURCH BULLETINS AND BLOOMERS

1. Chapel notice board: The Rev — will preach in this church on Sunday next at 11.

Don't worry; it may never happen.

☆

2. Sign on a church Bulletin board, in Benten, Wisconsin: For God so loved the world that He didn't send a committee.

☆

3. Sign on a church lawn in Des Moines, Iowa: Keep off the grass. That means you.

☆

4. Sign in front of Chicago church: The competition is terrible, but we're still open for business.

☆

5. Sign outside a Dallas church: Last chance to pray before entering the freeway.

☆

6. Sign on a church bulletin board in Denver: If you have trouble, come in and tell us about them. If you have none, come in and tell us how you do it.

☆

7. Notice in a church bulletin: The Lord loveth a cheerful giver. He also accepts from a grouch.

☆

8. Announcement on the bulletin board of a church in Ohio: This is segregated church — for sinners only. All welcome.

☆

9. Sign on a church in Atlanta: Come to church next Sunday. If you know no sins, bring someone who has.

10. Sign outside a Louisiana church: Heaven knows when you were here last.

☆

11. Sign outside a church in Dallas: Join our sit-in demonstration every Sunday.

☆

12. Bulletin item: The only organised senior choir will sing for the time at the morning service, and a real threat is anticipated.

☆

13. Church Bulletin: The high school choir has been disbanded for the summer with the thanks of the church.

☆

14. Church Bulletin: We are happy to welcome Rev Gylliam Jansors a sour speaker this morning.

☆

15. A church bulletin board carried this announcement: Special speaker at noon meetings each Wednesday in Lent will be Dr P. O. Misque the highest paid clergyman in New England.

☆

16. Church Bulletin: A new loudspeaker has been installed in the church auditorium: It was given by one of the deacons in honour of his wife.

☆

17. The Curate reading the church notices: Next Sunday is Easter. Those ladies who have eggs please lay them in the church porch.

☆

18. The young mothers meet each Wednesday. Will those who wish to become young mothers, please meet me in the vestry any Thursday evening.

☆

19. From a Winsted, Connecticutt church Bulletin: Pot luck supper. Prayer and Medication follow.

20. From a church Bulletin: Mr Solomon is conducting the evening lethargy, at 9:30.

☆

21. Absence: I shall be away from the parish attending the diocesan church school from April 21-24. It will be convenient if parishioners will abstain from arranging to be buried or from making other calls during this time.

☆

22. Parish Magazine: Mr Parker was elected and has accepted the office of Peoples Church Warden. We could not get a better man.

☆

23. Church Magazine: The Chairman of the Urban District Council with members and officers of the council and their wives attended morning service, on Sunday June 26. The service was conducted by the Vicar who, as is usual on these occasions, looked at the Council and prayed for the town.

☆

24. Church Magazine: The Vicar returns home after a month's holiday. We look forward to seeing him much improved in every way.

☆

25. South London Paper: The other woman was placed on probation, in 1960 for stealing St Paul's Cathedral Churchyard, since then she had lived a respectable life.

☆

26. Church Magazine: On Sunday the Rector officiated and preached his farewell sermon. The choir rendered the anthem — O clap your hands together.

☆

27. Parish Magazine: A mission is not simply the work of the missionaries. We must all be behind them preparing the way for them.

28. St. John's Church, Sunday next at 6 P.M. PEARLS BEFORE SWINE. We should like to see you there.

☆

29. From a Bulletin: The church dinner was like heaven. Many we expected to see there were absent.

☆

30. In the bulletin of a Baltimore Church: January 21, 7 a.m. Methodist women will unite with Methodist men at breakfast. Followed by prayer and self-denial service.

☆

31. Sign on a bulletin board in a small town: SUBJECT FOR THIS SUNDAY:- DO YOU KNOW WHAT HELL IS LIKE? COME AND HEAR OUR ORGANIST.

☆

32. West Sussex County Times: I write in behalf of the church warden to state we think desirable to make a change in the arrangement for keeping the grass in order as Mr Basely is now getting infirm. We have given notice to expire at Christmas.

☆

33. The Rev Earl Devanny of Woodbridge, New Jersey advertised a sermon entitled "WHAT HEAVEN IS LIKE AND HOW TO GET IN." This drew only a moderate congregation. So the Minister thought hard and advertised another sermon for the following Sunday. The title was, "WHAT HELL IS LIKE AND HOW TO GET IN."

This time the response was so overwhelming that the church was filled to overflowing.

☆

34. New York Paper: POPE CITES DANGERS FACING THE WORLD. NAMES EIGHT CARDINALS.

☆

35. Maxy Paper: Cemetery:- We have carefully considered the fees charged for opening the closing graves and the

prices charged, for the sale of grave spaces and desire to call the attention of the council to the advisability of referring the matter to the Public Amusement Committee.

☆

36. "Change Your Wife Through Prayer" will be the sermon subject Sunday.

☆

37. Through radio and television, more people now learn of Christ each week than in the first 1.000 years before Christianity.

☆

38. Bishop Codman surprised the congregation of the Episcopal Church last Sunday. The Bishop preached a fine sermon.

☆

39. The Salem Mission Covenant Church of Penncock held its annual meeting on New Year's Day. Under the able leadership of our chairman, Albin Broberg business proceeded quickly and smoothly and the ladies took care of our physical needs not only once but twice during the day.

☆

40. Nobleair's Will Sin at Church of God.

☆

41. The annual Christmas party at the office will be hell tonight.

☆

42. ST JOHN BAPTIST CHURCH. Rev L.M. Brown Pastor: The members met with the pastor in bed in the pastor's home and had a lovely meeting; reports were good.

☆

43. Listing of sermon topics—
Morning: "All Men Seek Thee."
Evening: "Foolish Virgins.

44. The pastor will preach and there will be special sinning by the congregation.

☆

45. The Berean Bible Class will hold a sinner in the church on March 9. Tickets may be secured from members of the class.

☆

46. Elder Valese, pastor of the Soul Stirring Church, Brooklyn, will speak here at eight o'clock. She will bring a quart with her and they will sing appropriate selections during the service.

☆

The following bloomers were sent to me by Dr Raleigh H. Pickard, Penny Farms, Florida, United States of America.

47. This afternoon there will be a baptismal in the South and the North ends of the Church. Children will be baptised at both ends.

☆

48. Tuesday at 4:00 PM there will be an ice cream social. All ladies giving milk, please come early.

☆

49. Wednesday, the Ladies Literary Society will meet. Mrs Johnson will sing, "Put me in my little bed" accompanied by the pastor.

☆

50. This morning, a special collection will be taken to defray the expense on the new carpet. All wishing to do something on the carpet, please come forward and get a piece of paper.

☆

51. The ladies of the Church have cast off clothing of every kind and they may be seen in the Church basement on Friday afternoon.

☆

52. This evening at 7 PM there will be hymn singing in the park across the Church. Bring a blanket and come prepared to sin.

57

11
CHURCH COLLECTIONS & OFFERINGS

1. The collection is a church function in which many take a passing interest.

☆

2. The way some people give, you would think the church is coin operated.

☆

3. Some people will bring a hymnbook or a prayerbook but not a pocket book to a church.

☆

4. It's funny how a dollar can look so big when you take it to the church and so small when you take it to the supermarket.

☆

5. Anybody who thinks there's a shortage of coins hasn't been to church lately.

☆

6. If there is no hell, many preachers are obtaining money under false pretense.

☆

7. It is impossible to preach with one eye on the conscience and the other on the collection.

☆

8.   A big silver dollar, a little brown cent,
     Rolling along together they went,
     Rolling along the smooth sidewalk,
     when the dollar remarked for the dollar can talk:

     "You poor little cent, you cheap little mite,
     I'm bigger and more than twice as bright,

I'm worth more than you a hundredfold,
and written in letters bold,
Is the motto drawn from the pious creed,
In God we trust, which all can read.

"Yes, I know" said the cent. "I am a cheap little mite,
And know I'm not big, nor good, nor bright,
And yet," said the cent, with a meek little sigh;
"You don't go to church as often as I."

☆

9. "When I look at this congregation," the minister told the audience, "I ask myself, 'where are the poor?'"

"But then, when I look at the collection, I say to myself, 'Where are the rich?'"

☆

10. Dean Swift was asked to preach a sermon on behalf of Dublin charity and the organisers dropped a hint that on previous occasions preachers had somewhat prejudiced their cause by speaking too long.

"I shall be short," said the Dean. When he entered the pulpit, he said, "My text is 'He that giveth unto the poor, lendeth unto the Lord'. Brethren, you have heard the terms of the loan. If you are satisfied with security, down with the dust."

That was all. The collection was a record one.

☆

11. Andrew Carnegie, the steel magnate, once attended a tiny village church in the mountains of Caucasus. When the collection was taken, the millionaire philanthropist put a hundred dollar bill in it.

Conforming to custom the village priest announced the total of the collection. "Brethren," he said, "the collection today amounts to three roubles and twenty copecks, and if the note the stranger has given is genuine, we shall have another 100 dollars. Brethren, let us pray that it is."

☆

12. Dr Joseph Parker, famous preacher at the city

59

Temple, once announced to his vast congregation that the collection would be for widows and orphans and if there were any among the congregation that day they would not be expected to contribute.

The next Sunday, he referred to the collection, reminding hearers that he had told widows and orphans that they would not be expected to contribute. Then, after a sinister pause, he added: "Never bloody battle produced so many widows and orphans as did my announcement."

☆

13. "Brethren," said a Negro pastor, "brethren, I have got a five-dollar sermon, and a two-dollar sermon, and a one-dollar sermon. I want this here meretricious congregation to take up a collection as to which one of them they can afford to hear."

☆

14. Three Scotchmen were in church one Sunday morning when the pastor made a strong appeal for some worthy cause, hoping that everyone in the church would give at least two dollars each or more. The three Scots became very nervous as the collection plate neared them when one of them fainted and the other two carried him out.

☆

15. A church was having difficulty in getting money from its members to pay for the mortgage on its new Sunday school building, even though the folks kept on informing the pastor they were praying for the completion of the structure. So one Sunday morning the offering suddenly skyrocketed when this slogan appeared on all collection plates:

"Pay now, pray later."

☆

16. The preacher passed the hat after the sermon. When it was returned to him without a penny in it, he turned it upside down to show the congregation the emptiness of it. Then he raised his eyes upward and exclaimed, "I thank God. I was able to get my hat back from this congregation."

17. The pastor of a small church in Southern Italy ended his sermon with the following observations: "At the door, as usual, there will be some one to accept your gifts. I should like to remind you, my dear brethren, that the anatomical construction of the angels precludes their use of your pant button contributions."

☆

18. An Orthodox priest, a Catholic priest and a Rabbi are talking about how much of the collections they give God, and how much they keep for themselves.

"I divide all money coming into the church into a big pile and a small pile, the big one is for God and the small one for me" says the Orthodox priest. "Well," says the Catholic priest, "I divide the money into two even piles, one for God and one for me."

"I put all the money on a tray and throw it up into the air," says the Rabbi. "And what God wants, God keeps."

☆

19. The minister arose to address his congregation. "There is a certain man among us today who is flirting with another man's wife. Unless he puts five dollars in the collection box, his name will be read from the pulpit."

When the collection plate came, there were nineteen five dollar bills and a two dollar one with this note attached "Other three pay day."

☆

20. This is one of Mark Twain's stories:

"Some years ago in Hartford, we all went to church one hot sweltering night to hear the annual report of Mr Hawley, a city missionary who went around finding people who needed help and didn't want to ask for it. He told of the life in cellars, where poverty resided, he gave instances of heroism and devotion of the poor. When a man with millions gives, he said, we make a great deal of noise. It's a noise in the wrong place for it's the widow's mite that counts.

"Well, Hawley worked me up to a great pitch. I could hardly wait for him to get through. I had $400 in my pocket. I wanted to give that and borrow more to give. You could see

61

the greenbacks in every eye. But instead of passing the plate to the crowd then, he kept on talking and talking and talking, and as he talked, it grew hotter and hotter and we grew sleepier and sleepier and sleepier. My enthusiasm went down, down, down $100 at a clip — until finally, when the plate did come around, I stole ten cents out of it."

☆

21. The preacher was at ease after Sunday service.
"Many folks in church?" asked his wife.
"Yes, good attendance and a stranger was present, but I did not see him."
"But how do you know?"
"There was a dollar bill in the contribution box."

☆

22. "I've been racking my mind, but I can't place you," one man said to another at a gathering. "And you look very much like somebody I have seen a lot, somebody I don't like but I can't tell you why. Isn't that strange?"

"Nothing strange about it," the other said. "You have seen me a lot, and I know why you resent me. For two years I have passed you the collection plate in our church!"

☆

23. An old timer these days is one who can remember when he put a quarter in the collection plate and felt a philanthropist.

☆

24. An elderly woman was seated in church next to a small boy. When the collection plate was passed, she began fumbling through her cluttered purse. The boy nudged her. "You take my dime," he said, "and I'll hide under the seat."

☆

25. As the offering plates were being passed at church, a small boy seated with his father blurted out: "Don't pay for me, dad, I'm under five."

☆

26. Bennett Cerf, in his book, THE SOUND OF LAUGH-

TER, tells about old lady Abernathy who hadn't seen her young grandson since his christening. And when she heard he was being sent to her country place to spend his ninth birthday with her, "She was so delighted she put five dollars in the collection plate that Sunday at church. The next Sunday after her grandson went home she put in ten dollars."

☆

27. After the sermon on free salvation, the minister of a southern black church announced that the collection would be taken by Brother Martin. One of the congregation rose in the back of the church, however, and said, "Parson, you all done said that salvation was free — free as the water we drink."

"Yes, brother," agreed the minister. "Salvation is free, but when we pipes it to you, you gotta pay for the piping."

☆

28. A salesman's son bragged, "All my father has to do is to sell a car and he makes fifty dollars." A second boy, whose father was a lawyer, said "That's nothing. My father merely tenders advice, and he collects five hundred dollars." And the third boy, whose father was a minister, boasted, "My father gives a talk and it takes ten people to take up the collection."

☆

29. A mother was grumbling after church service that the church was not air-conditioned, the choir sang horribly and the sermon was tedious, whereupon her seven-year-old son said, "Mom, what do you expect for the dime you put in the collection plate?"

☆

30. A young boy who was starting out for church one morning, was given two dimes, one for the collection plate and one for himself. As he was walking down the street he played with the coins. One of them slipped out of hand, rolled away into a sewer. The boy gazed sadly into the sewer and then said, "Well, there goes the Lord's dime."

☆

31. The deacon was passing the plate in the church. A woman hurried in, dropped a coin into the plate, and moved

to a seat. The deacon was at the last pew when the woman was bustling back. She snatched the coin from the plate and started for the door. The deacon stopped her. "Look here," he said. "Why do you come in here, drop a coin in the plate, then take it out again?"

The woman shook him off indignantly and exclaimed, "I got into the wrong church."

12

CLERGY VS CLERGY

1. The Reverend, Jacob and John were colleagues in an old church. One Sunday when it was Rev John's turn to preach, it happened that he got drenched by a heavy shower and was standing before the vestry fire drying his clothes when Dr Jacob, came in, whom he requested to take his place, as he had escaped the rain.

"No, Sir," said Jacob, "preach yourself; you will be dry though in the pulpit."

☆

2. A conceited young clergyman delivered a sermon and sought his bishop's opinion of it.

"Well," said the bishop, "since you ask me, I think your sermon resembled the great sword of Charlemagne."

"It was a victorious sword, was it not?" replied the young man, deeply flattered.

"Yes," said the bishop, "it was. But it was also long and flat."

☆

3. A young clergyman was 'in retreat' at a country house near Guildford and was not supposed to leave the house or its grounds without the permission of his superiors. Nevertheless he decided, one fine afternoon, to play truant and set out on foot for Guildford, but had the bad luck to encounter his bishop, who asked him what he was doing away from his place of retreat and whether he had obtained leave of absence.

"No, my Lord," answered the young man, "but I was moved by the Holy Spirit to go and do some shopping in Guildford."

"Indeed," replied the bishop, "then all I can say is that either you or the Holy Spirit is in error. I live in Guildford and happen to know that today is early closing day."

4. The rector of a fashionable New York church was induced to preach at a well-known prison. When in the vestry, he said to the prison chaplain, "Now I have come, I don't know what to say to your convicts."

The chaplain replied, "Preach to them exactly as you do to your own congregation; and remember only one thing — my people have been found out and yours have not been yet."

☆

5. A lady who was a great admirer of a certain preacher took a bishop with her to hear him, and asked him afterwards what he thought of the sermon.

"It was a long one," said the bishop.

"Yes," said the lady, "but there was a saint in the pulpit."

"And a martyr in the pew," rejoined the bishop.

☆

6. "With your ready speech," remarked a young minister to a senior clergyman, "I wonder why you spend so much time on your sermons. Many's the time I've written a sermon and caught a salmon before breakfast."

"Well," replied the elder clergyman, "all I can say is, I'd rather have eaten your salmon than listened to your sermon."

☆

7. A retired bishop was once asked by a newly ordained preacher, "What should I preach about?"

The elderly man thought a moment, then replied, "Preach about God and preach about twenty minutes."

☆

8. A young preacher in the midst of ministers and laymen spoke about how grateful he was that he had never come into contact with college, especially seminary. He admitted he had no education and seemed proud of it.

An old pastor asked, "Do I understand you correctly? Are you saying that you are thankful for your ignorance? If so, you have a great deal to be thankful for."

9. A pompous Bishop of Oxford was once stopped on a London street by a rugged urchin.

"Well my little man, and what can I do for you?" inquired the churchman.

"The time of day, please, your lordship."

With considerable difficulty the portly bishop extracted his timepiece. "It is exactly half past five, my lad."

"Well," said the boy, setting his feet for a good start, "at half past six you go to hell." — and he was off like a flash and around the corner. The bishop flushed and furious, his watch dangling from its chain, floundered wildly after him.

But as he rounded the corner he ran plump into the outstretched arms of the venerable Bishop of London. "Oxford, Oxford," remonstrated that surprised dignitary.

"Why this unseemly haste?"

Puffing, blowing, spluttering, the outraged Bishop gasped out; "That young ragamuffin — I told him it was half past five-he-er-told me to go to hell at half past six."

"Yes, yes," said the Bishop of London with suspicion of a twinkle in his kindly eyes, "but why such haste? You've got almost an hour."

☆

10. Two pastors were discussing the problems in their respective churches.

"I don't know how to get all my members involved in the Lord's work," moaned one of them. "I have tried for years, but only ten per cent of them have time for christian work."

"That's terrible," sympathised his friend. "In my church all 100% of the members are working actively.

"Why, wonderful" exclaimed the other. "How on earth did you manage?"

"Simple," was the reply, "Fifty per cent of the members are working for me and fifty per cent are against me."

☆

11. Here is a story of a Negro clergyman who pestered his bishop with appeals for help that it became necessary to tell him that he must not send any more appeals.

The Negro clergyman's next communication was as follows:- "This is not an appeal. It is a report. I have no pants."

☆

12. The bishop had occasion to chide a clergyman for the worldliness of his riding to hounds. "It's not a bit more worldly," said the clergyman, "than a ball in Buckingham Palace which your Lordship recently attended."

"But I was never nearer than three rooms from dancing," explained the bishop.

"Oh, well, if it comes to that," retorted the unrepentent clergyman, "I'm never within three fields of the hounds."

☆

13. A minister wrote to his bishop asking if his Lordship could come and conduct a quiet Day in the parish.

The bishop, after looking up the record of the parish, replied, "Your parish does not need a quiet day; it wants an earthquake."

☆

14. A CLERGYMAN'S LETTER TO THE BISHOP:- "Sometime ago I wrote to inform you that one of our boys who was confirmed in January took his confirmation gift money and bought a collared lizard which he named Bishop in your honour. A little later he bought a smaller lizard and named it Rector in my honour. I thought you would be interested to know that I recently learned that the Bishop ate the Rector."

DENOMINATIONS

1. A group of world leaders in the Presbyterian Church, met in Scotland for a Conference — and on a warm summer's afternoon went to explore the beautiful countryside. Coming to a temporary bridge that spanned a swift-running stream, they started confidently to cross it. When they were half way over, the bridge keeper suddenly appeared and hollered that the bridge had been declared unsafe. The spokesman for the church party didn't quite hear the keeper's admonition and called back, "It's all right, my friend, we are Presbyterians from the Conference."

The bridge keeper replied, "If ye dinna get off the bridge this minute, you'll all be Baptists."

☆

2. The new Vicar called by mistake on a family of Baptists the other day, and when little Cecil opened the door, the Vicar asked why Cecil and his mother and father did not come to church on Sundays.

"We don't belong to your abomination," was little Cecil's reply.

☆

3. The mayor of a tough border town was about to engage a preacher for the new church. "Parson, you aren't by any chance a Baptist, are you?"

"No, Sir."

"Well. I was just going to say that we have to haul our water twelve miles."

☆

4. A Baptist deacon had advertised a cow for sale. "How much are you asking for it?" inquired a prospective buyer.

"A hundred and fifty dollars," replied the advertiser.

"And how much milk does she give?"

"Four gallons a day," he replied.

"But how do I know she'll actually give that amount?"

asked the purchaser.

"Oh, you can trust me," he explained, "I am a Baptist deacon."

"I will buy it," answered the other. "I'll take the cow home and bring back the money later. You can trust me, I'm a Presbyterian elder."

When the deacon arrived home, he asked his wife, "What's a Presbyterian elder?"

"Oh," she explained, "a Presbyterian elder is about the same as a Baptist deacon."

"Oh, dear," groaned the deacon, "I've lost my cow."

☆

5. The Baptist, the Presbyterian and the Lutheran were left legacies by a friend on condition that each should put five pounds in the coffin. The Baptist put in a five-pound note. The Presbyterian put in a five-pound note which he borrowed from the Baptist. The Lutheran took out the two five-pound notes and put in a cheque for fifteen pounds, payable to bearer.

Three days later, he was astonished to learn the cheque had been presented and cashed. The undertaker was a Methodist.

☆

6. A Baptist family had a death in the family while their minister was out of town. They asked the local Methodist minister to conduct the funeral service.

He called his bishop and asked. "Can I bury a Baptist?"

The bishop quickly replied, "Sure, bury all the Baptists you can!"

☆

7. Get religion like a Methodist
    Experience it like a Baptist
    Stick to it like a Lutheran
    Conciliate it like a Congregationalist
    Be proud of it like an Episcopalian
    Simplify it like a Jew
    Pay for it like a Presbyterian
    Practise it like the Salvation Army

70

Propagate it like a Roman Catholic
Enjoy it like a Negro.

☆

8. The Baptist and Christian Churches were trying to merge. All the members of both Churches agreed, except one old-timer.

"No," he said, as he shook his head.

"Why, Sir?" asked a preacher.

"Well, my mother and father were Baptists, my grandparents were Baptists, all of my people were Baptists, and nobody is going to make a Christian out of me now!"

☆

9. An old Quaker farmer back in Oklahoma would never utter the name of the Lord in vain or use any abusive language. But one day his mule hitched to the hay wagon, wouldn't move even a little. The God-fearing farmer tried every means to persuade the beast to move, but to no avail. Finally, he held the end of the reins. "Mule," he said patiently in a low voice, "thee knows that because of my religion I cannot beat thee, or curse thee, or abuse thee in any way. But mule," he continued, "What thee do not know is that I can sell thee to a Methodist."

☆

10. A certain Presbyterian Church in New York was supposed to be aristocratic. Once the minister of this church was accosted by a parishioner after a sermon. "Parson, is it possible for a man to achieve salvation outside of Presbyterian church?

The parson replied superciliously, "It is conceivable that such a possibility might exist. However, no gentleman would avail of it."

☆

11. One summer, the Baptists, the Methodists and the Presbyterians agreed to conduct an evangelical revival week. At the end of the week, the ministers got together to know the results of the camp Bible session.

The Baptist said, "We got six new members."

71

The Methodist said, "We did even better. Nine people became converts to the Methodist faith."

They both turned to the Presbyterian and asked him how he fared.

The Presbyterian answered, "We did much better than you two. We didn't convert any but we happily got rid of fifteen reprobates."

☆

12. A newly appointed Episcopalian Minister was conducting a survey of his parish. When stopped at the Bohr farm, Mrs Bohr answered the door. "Good morning, sister," said he, "do you have any Episcopalians here?"

"Episcopalians?" said Mrs B. with a bewildered look. "Wait a minute, I ask my husband." She called back into the house, "Honey, what was that creature you shot back of the barn last week?"

☆

13. While in a rural area, a candidate for political office sought to determine the denominational sympathies of his audience. Adjusting his tie and clearing his throat, he pontificated: "My great-grandfather was an Episcopalian (stony silence), but my great-grandmother belonged to the Congregational Church (continued silence). My grandfather was a Baptist (more silence) but my grandmother was a Presbyterian (still rigid silence). But I had a great-aunt who was a Methodist (loud applause). And I have always followed the religion of my great-aunt (loud and continuous cheers). He was elected.

14
DOZING IN CHURCH

1. It's disconcerting to fall asleep in church and have a fly buzz into one's open mouth.

☆

2. Some churches seem to be sound in doctrine, but they are also sound asleep.

☆

3. All church buildings should be air-conditioned; it is unhealthy to sleep in a stuffy room.

☆

4. Many churches are now serving coffee after the service. Presumably this is to get the people thoroughly awake before they start to drive home.

☆

5. When people go to sleep in church, somebody should wake up the preacher.

☆

6. Preachers don't talk in their sleep, but they talk in other people's sleep.

☆

7. Satan is never too busy to rock the cradle of a sleeping Christian.

☆

8. A good sermon helps in two ways. Some rise from it greatly strengthened. Others wake from it greatly refreshed.

☆

9. A preacher confessed to bouts of insomnia, then added, "But I have a sure-fire remedy. When I wake up in the night and can't get back to sleep, I go over some of my sermons in my mind. I find that my sermons have the same effect on me that they had on some of the members in my congregation."

10. A clergyman told from his text
    How Samson was scissored and vexed;
    Then a barber arose,
    From his sweet Sunday doze,
    Got rattled, and shouted, "Who's next?"

☆

11. The head of a civilian defence corps looked up the parish priest. "We're planning on simulating a bombing, Father. How many people could sleep in your church if they were bombed out of their homes?"

"I don't know how many could lie down and sleep, but every Sunday about 900 persons sleep here sitting upright."

☆

12. "Did you hear Robinson snoring in church this morning? It was simply awful."

"Yes, I did — he woke me up."

☆

13. The minister called on Mrs Macshoddie. "By the way," he remarked after a while, "I was sorry to see your husband leave church last Sunday right in the middle of my sermon. I trust nothing was seriously the matter with him?"

"Oh, no sir," replied Mrs Macshoddie. "It was nothing very serious; but you see, the poor man does have a habit of walking in his sleep."

☆

14. The clergyman's eloquence may have been at fault, still he felt annoyed to find that an old gentleman fell asleep during the sermon on two consecutive Sundays. So, after service on the second week, he told the boy who accompanied the sleeper that he wished to speak to him in the vestry.

"My boy," said the minister, when they were closetted together, "Who is that elderly gentleman you attend church with?"

"Grandpa," was the reply.

"Well," said the clergyman, "if you will only keep him awake during my sermon, I'll give you a nickel each week."

The boy fell in with the arrangement, and for the next

74

two weeks the old gentleman listened attentively to the sermon. The third week, however, found him soundly asleep.

The vexed clergyman sent for the boy and said, "I am very angry with you. Your grandpa was asleep again today. Didn't I promise you a nickel to keep him awake?"

"Yes," replied the boy, "but grandpa now gives me a dime not to disturb him."

☆

15. A little boy in church, who had just been aroused from his nap, said to his father, "Daddy, has he finished?"

The father replied, "He's finished, but he isn't stopped yet."

☆

16. A parson looking up from the sermon he was reading, was horrified to see his son in the gallery pelting the congregation with small pebbles. Before he could get out a word of reproach, the young son said, "You tend to your sermon, Daddy, and I will keep the congregation awake."

☆

17. The pastor finally decided he must talk to the richest member of the congregation, no matter how much it hurt.

"Why," he asked the rich man, "do you fall asleep when I am delivering my message?"

Answered the rich man, "Would I fall asleep if I didn't trust you?"

☆

18. Some go to church to see and to be seen,
Some go there to say they have been
Some go there to sleep and nod,
But few go there to worship God.

☆

19. I cannot praise the preacher's eyes,
I never saw his glance divine,
He always shuts them when he prays,
And when he preaches he shuts mine.

20. A preacher, who had succeeded in putting an elderly man to sleep with his sermon was preaching hard for a decision. He pounded on the pulpit and almost shouted as he said, "Those who want to go to hell stand up, and I mean stand up!" The old man was awakened by the thunderous words, "Stand up" and he did. He looked around a bit and said. "Preacher, I don't know what we are voting on, but it looks like you and I are the only ones for it."

☆

21. Pastor: "What do we learn from the story of Eutyches, the young man who, listening to the preaching of Apostle Paul, fell asleep and fell out of a window to his death?"

Minister: "Ministers should learn not to preach too long sermons."

☆

22. A minister and an agnostic often indulged in friendly discussion of views. After much urging, the agnostic finally agreed to attend a church service the following Sunday. The minister prepared a masterly discourse, to appeal especially to his friend's appreciation of logic.

When the two met on Monday, the agnostic conceded: "I'll say this for your Sunday sermon: it kept me awake until the early hours of the morning."

The clergyman beamed. "I am happy that I succeeded in making you doubt the wisdom of your convictions."

"Oh," said the other, "it wasn't that. You see, when I nap in the daytime I can't sleep at night."

15

EPITAPHS

1. **EPITAPH FOR A GODLY MAN'S TOMB**
Here lies a piece of Christ: a star in dust;
A vein of gold; a china dish that must
Be used in heaven, when God shall feast the just.
— *Robert Wild*

☆

2. **ON THE CLERGY OF A COUNTRY PARISH**
Here lies, within his tomb, so calm
Old Giles: Pray sound his knell;
Who thought no song was like a psalm,
No music like a bell.
— *William Shenstone*

☆

3. **EPITAPH ON AN IRISH PRIEST**
Here I lie for the last time,
Lying has been my pastime,
And now I've joined the Heavenly choir,
I hope I still may play the Lyre.

☆

4. **EPITAPH UPON A PURITANICAL
LOCKSMITH**
A zealous locksmith died of late,
And did arrive at heaven's gate,
He stood without and would not knock,
Because he meant to pick the lock.

☆

5. **EPITAPH**
Here lies the man who stripp'd sin bare,
And kept lean, on hard earn'd fare;
Who forc'd the poor at home stay,
But rode to church on Sabbath day;
And went to heav'n the sinless way,
Because he bother'd God with prayer,
And would not let him have his way.

6. **ON THE REVEREND JONATHAN DOE**
Here lies the Reverend Jonathan Doe
Where he has gone to I don't know;
If haply to the realms above,
Farewell to happiness and love,
If haply to a lower level,
I can't congratulate the devil.

☆

7. **EPITAPH ON A DOCTOR OF DIVINITY**
Here lies a Doctor of Divinity,
He was a fellow of Trinity;
He knew as much about Divinity
As other fellows do of Trinity.

— *Richard Porson*

☆

8. **EPITAPH ON CARDINAL WOLSEY**
Begot by Butchers, but by Bishops bred,
How high his honour holds his haughty head!

☆

9. **EPITAPH**
Here I lie at the church door,
Here I lie because I am poor,
When I rise at the Judgement Day,
I shall be as warm as they.

☆

10. **EPITAPH ON LORD PETER ROBINSON**
Here lies the Christian, judge and poet Peter,
Who broke the laws of God, man and metre.

— *John Gibson Lockhart*

☆

11. **EPITAPH ON DEAN INGE**
Hark! the herald angels sing,
Timidly, because Dean Inge
Has arrived and seems to be
Bored with immortality.

12. ON A PASTOR'S TOMB
Go tell the Church I'm dead
But they need shed no tears
For though I am dead I'm no more dead
Than they have been for years.

☆

13. ROBERT WOLFE WHO PERCEIVED AN UNPLEASANT STREAK OF ANTISEMITISM IN CHESTERTON'S VIEWS, PROPOSED THIS EPITAPH
Here lies Mr Chesterton
Who to Heaven might have gone
But didn't when he heard the news
That the place was run by Jews.

☆

14. EPITAPH ON THE WIFE OF THE PARISH CLERK
The children of Israel wanted bread,
And the Lord he sent them manna
Old clerk Wallace wanted a wife,
And the devil sent him Anna.

☆

15. EPITAPH ON A PARISH CLERK
There lies entombed within this vault so dark,
A tailor, clothdraw'r, soldier, and a clerk,
Death snatched him hence, and also from him took,
His needle, thimble, sword, and prayer book.
He could not work nor fight, what then?
He left the world, and faintly cry'd—Amen.

☆

16.
Here lies William Smith,
And what is rarish,
He was born, bred, and
Hanged in this parish.

☆

17.
Never missed a Sunday's Service
Present at 5013 Christenings,
Present at 2112 marriages,
Present at 4699 funerals.

18. Keep death and Judgement always in your eye,
Or else the devil off with you will fly,
And in his kiln with brimstone ever fry,
If you neglect the narrow road to seek,
Christ will reject you, like a half-burnt brick.

☆

19. **TO THE MEMORY OF THOMAS MANSE**
"Lord, the grass is free—why not for me?"
(A creditor who was ruined by Mr Manse wrote
under it.)
And the Lord answered and said,
"Because thy debts ain't paid."

☆

20. **REV JOHN TYRWITT, 1928**
Here lies John Tyrwitt,
A learned divine,
He died in a fit
Through drinking port wine.

☆

21. **TRUTH & FICTION**
Here lies Rev A.B.
For many years Missionary in B-district.
He was accidentally shot by his native servant,
"WELL DONE, THOU GOOD AND FAITHFUL
SERVANT."

☆

22. Here lies cut down like unripe fruit
The wife of Deacon Amos Shute,
She died of drinking too much coffee
Anno Domini eighteen forty.

☆

23. The Dame, who lies within this tomb
Had Rachel's charms and Leah's fruitful womb,
Ruth's filial love, and Lydia's faithful heart,
Martha's just care, and Mary's better part.

16
EVANGELISTS

1. D.L. Moody, the famous evangelist, had just finished preaching a passionate sermon on the salvation of God in London when a well-known English grammarian came to him and said, "Moody, you ought to be ashamed of yourself. Tonight, you massacred the English language unforgivably. Do you realise that you made 45 grammatical errors in your 30-minute sermon?"

Moody replied, "I'm sorry, Sir. But may I say something? With my limited knowledge I have come here to preach the Gospel, and souls are being saved. What are you doing with your perfect command of the King's English?"

☆

2. The open-air evangelist warning his hearers to escape the wrath of God, said that they had been fully warned of the perils of sin. "Without doubt," he said, "on the Day of Judgement there would be weeping and gnashing of teeth."

"But I ain't have teeth," said a little woman.

"Never mind," the evangelist shouted, "teeth will be provided."

☆

3. A young skeptic in the congregation interrupted Billy Sunday with the question, "Who was Cain's wife?"

The evangelist cooly replied, "I honour every seeker after knowledge of the truth. But I have a word of warning for this questioner. Don't risk losing salvation by too much inquiry after other men's wives."

☆

4. The Reverend George Whitefield remarked in a sermon that all God made was perfect. At this a man who had a hunchback, rose from the pew and asked, "What do you think of me?"

"Think of you," said the great evangelist, "Why, Sir, you are the most perfect hunchback my eyes ever beheld."

81

5. Billy Sunday, it is said, sometimes took other preachers' sermons and preached them. Once after he had preached one of Gypsy Smith's sermons, Gypsy took him to task. "You preached my sermon almost word to word," he accused Sunday.

"But after you preached that night when I heard you," said Sunday, "you sang 'pass it on' and that's what I am doing."

☆

6. A man once came to Gypsy Smith and told him that although he had gone through the Bible several times, he had received no inspiration from it.

Gypsy Smith replied, "Let it go through you once, and you will tell a different story!"

☆

7. Dr E. Stanley Jones, the well-known evangelist, tells of the frustrating experience he once had with an interpreter who bungled his whole message. Feeling utterly dejected and desolate, Dr Jones asked God, "Why did you allow that confounded interpreter to spoil my message and my whole night?"

The Lord told him: "Stanley, this is precisely what you have sometimes done with my message. Think of the many many times you have failed to convey fully or clearly what I wanted you to say."

☆

8. C.H. Spurgeon once asked a student for the ministry to preach an impromptu sermon. The result merits an entry in the GUINNESS BOOK OF RECORDS for the shortest sermon ever. Appropriately, it was on the subject of Zacchaeus, and this is how it went:

'First, Zacchaeus was a man of very small stature; so am I. Second, Zacchaeus was very much up a tree; so am I.' With that, the student sat down to shouts of 'More, more!' from his fellows.

"No," said Spurgeon, 'he could not improve upon that if he tried."

9. Many years ago, a woman was at a mission meeting led by the preacher Gipsy Smith. She wrote to him afterwards: 'Dear Sir, I feel that God is calling me to preach the Gospel. The trouble is, I have twelve children. What shall I do?'

Gipsy replied: 'Dear Madam, I am delighted to hear that God has called you to preach the Gospel. I am even more delighted to hear that he has provided you with a congregation.'

☆

10. Spurgeon told a story of a young pastor who was called upon to preach his first funeral sermon when the deacon of his church died. He hunted frantically for an appropriate verse, and finally found one that he thought would be suitable.

The small group looked up expectantly when he began to read his text: "And it came to pass that the beggar died."

☆

11. Billy Graham tells the story of a coach who was most eager for a certain ball player to be accepted by the college, so he arranged for an interview between the athlete and the dean. "If you are able to answer one simple question, you can enter college," said the dean. Then he asked, "How much is six and six?"

The athlete thought for a minute and he answered, "Thirteen."

There was silence. Then the coach broke in, "Ah, dean, let him in. He only missed it by two."

☆

12. When D.L. Moody was holding a series of meetings in a church on the outskirts of London, England, a minister, called on to pray, went on longer than the evangelist wished. So, in a firm but kind voice Moody announced, "While the good pastor is finishing his prayer, we will sing a hymn."

☆

13. When young and just converted, D.L. Moody used to fill up a pew in a rather aristocratic Boston church with street urchins. Many of the upper-crust church members resented this intrusion. When Moody tried to join the church, the board

discouraged him. "Think it over for a month," they advised. "And pray about it, too."

They thought that would be the last they would see Moody. But they failed to take into account his indomitable drive, for next month he appeared before the board again. Rather taken aback, they asked,

"Did you do what we suggested? Did you pray about it?"

"I did," Moody quietly replied.

"And did the Lord give you any encouragement?"

"Yes," said Moody, "He told me not to feel bad because He has been trying to get into this same church for the last twenty-five years, too."

☆

14. In one of his REVIVAL Meetings Billy Sunday requested all the couples present who had never quarrelled to come before him. A motley crowd of couples appeared before him, and Billy held his hands over their heads as if about to make a benediction, 'God bless these damned liars," he said.

Billy Graham carries on in the tradition of Billy Sunday. At a large public meeting in London he asked all those to stand up who were trying to live the life which would get them to heaven. A lot of people got up on their feet, but there was one little man in the front who remained seated.

"What's the matter with you?" he asked. "Don't you wish to go to heaven?"

Billy's exultation was suddenly broken off and there was complete silence.

"Not immediately," said the man with an air of conviction.

☆

15. When Billy Graham was conducting revival meetings in Glasgow, in Scotland, a reporter asked him, "How do you account for your success?"

"The only explanation I know," said the great evangelist, "is God".

"But why," asked the reporter, "did He choose you?"

"When I get to Heaven," said Billy Graham, "That's the first question I am going to ask Him."

16. James W. Cox once said to a friend of his, "Charles Haddon Spurgeon — What do you think of when I mention that name?"

"Well, it may be the devil in me, but this is what I think of: He had a beard, he smoked a cigar, and he was unordained. In South Texas, where I'm from, all three are sins for a preacher."

☆

17. D.L. Moody once entered a drug store distributing tracts. At the back of the store sat a gentleman reading a newspaper. Moody approached him and threw one of the temperance tracts before him. The old gentleman glanced at the tract and then looking benignly at Moody asked, "Are you a reformed drunkard?"

"No, Sir, I am not," cried Moody drawing back.

"Then why don't you reform?" quietly asked the gentleman.

☆

18. Bishop James K. Mathews, Washington wrote to me: I'm glad to know that you know my father-in-law (Dr E. Stanley Jones, the great evangelist and missionary to India). You may know that in 1971 I presided for a session of the South India Conference. I read out the appointments. For E. Stanley Jones I read: 'Ambassador Extraordinary and Minister Plenipotentiary of the Kingdom of God'."

17
EVE-TEASING

1. God created the world and rested,
   God created man and rested
   But after God created woman,
   Neither God nor man has rested.

☆

2. While walking in a cemetery, Jonah saw a man of the cloth standing over a grave and crying hysterically, "Why did you die, why did you die?" Being a Good Samaritan type, Jonah decided to try to comfort the minister and walked over. Observing the inscription on the tomb-stone, and seeing it was another man's grave, he said, "I am awfully sorry to see you so upset: This man must have been very close to you."

The Minister stopped crying for a moment, wiped his tears with his handkerchief and answered. "I never even saw him. He was my wife's first husband."

☆

3. A skeptic called on a minister to seek clarification on a point in the Holy Bible. "It puzzles me," he said, "when God tested Job, He took away everything from him but left him his wife. Why?"

"That's simple," said the minister. "After God finished testing Job, He returned unto him twice what He had taken away. If Job's wife had been taken away, He would have had to give him two wives. And such a penalty not even God dared to inflict on him."

☆

4. The ambitious woman somehow managed to get an invitation to an important function. She found herself seated between a renowned bishop and a distinguished Rabbi, and thought it would be ostentatious if she made the most out of this remarkable company.

"I feel," she said, "as if I were a leaf between the Old and the New Testaments."

"That page, madam," said the Rabbi, "is usually blank."

5. Once a Mormon preacher argued with Mark Twain on the subject of polygamy. After a long and vehement debate, the Mormon finally said, "Can you show me a single verse from the Holy Bible which forbids polygamy?"

"Certainly," replied the inimitable humorist, "No man can serve two masters."

☆

6. A backslider whose riotous Saturday night escapades brought him fame of a kind, began faithfully attending church on Sunday mornings. The pastor was highly gratified and told him, "How wonderful it makes me see you at service with your good wife!"

"Well, preacher," said the prodigal, "it's a matter of choice. I'd rather hear your sermons than hers."

☆

7. A woman met the minister after the Sunday service, and thanked him for his fine sermon, "I found it so helpful," said she.

The minister replied, "I hope it will not prove so helpful as my last sermon you heard me preach."

"Why, what do you mean?" asked the woman in surprise.

"Well," said the minister, "that sermon lasted you three months."

☆

8. A young girl came to the priest and confessed that she had incurred the sin of vanity.

"What makes you think that?" asked the father confessor.

"Because every morning when I look into the mirror I think how beautiful I am."

"Never fear, my child," was the reassuring reply. "That isn't a sin, it's only a mistake."

☆

9. A bishop who had an ill-tempered wife, once caught a small boy stealing grapes in his garden. The prelate chided the boy sternly and concluded, "Do you know, my son, why I tell this? There is one before whom even I am a crawling worm. Do you know who it is?"

"Sure," said the boy promptly, "your wife."

87

10. Curate: So you really think you would have run through all your money had it not been for your wife?

Young Man: Sure of it.

Curate: And, my good man, how did she stop your spending it all?

Young Man: She spent it first.

☆

11. A boy wrote a composition on the subject of the Quakers, who he described as a sect who never quarrelled, never got into a fight, never clawed each other and never jawed back.

The composition contained a postscript in those words: "Pa's Quaker, but Ma ain't."

☆

12. The vicar, awarding prizes at the local dog show, was scandalized at the costumes worn by some younger members of the fair sex.

"Look at that youngster," said he, "the one with cropped hair, the cigarette and breeches, holding two pups. Is it a boy or a girl?"

"A girl," said his companion. "She is my daughter."

"My dear Sir," the vicar was flustered. "Do forgive me. I would never have been so outspoken had I known you were her father."

"I am not," said the other. "I'm her mother."

☆

13. Dr Samuel Johnson was famous for his sabre-stroke gibes. Once, when James Boswell told him that he had a few days ago heard a certain woman preaching a sermon, the witty Johnson said, "Sir, a woman preaching is like a dog's walking on his hind legs. It is not done well; but you are surprised to find it done at all."

☆

14. A minister lately returned from a long holiday trip on which he had been accompanied by his wife. At a prayer meeting shortly afterward an elder offered up thanks for the minister's safe return. "O Lord," he said, "we thank Thee for

bringing our pastor safe home, and his dear wife, too, O Lord, for Thou preservest man and beast."

☆

15. A lady whose husband's climb up the ladder of business led her to a more ritzy way of life changed to a better car, better home, better furs, and a better church. After another major advance which landed her in the Cadillac stage, she paid a visit to her latest minister. "I've had the feeling for some time that I should join you with my friends at the St Ritz Church," she said, swinging her furs around her back and flashing her two carot diamonds. "What would be your opinion, Sir?"

"My dear lady," the clergyman replied, "it matters little what kind of label you put on an empty bottle!"

☆

16. When a woman asked St Francis de Sales if it was a sin to use rouge, he replied, "Some theologians say so, others think it is a harmless practice."

"But" she gushed, "What do you advise me to do?"

"Why not follow a middle course" St Francis de Sales said, "and rouge only one cheek."

☆

17. "Minister, I believe the Bible says it's wrong to profit from other people's mistakes?"

"That's substantially correct, yes."

"In that case, how about refunding the twenty dollars I paid you for marrying us last year?"

☆

18. Aaron was very much upset when he came to know that Pharaoh had broken his promise to Moses for the second time to release the children of Israel from bondage. In desperation he said to his wife, "The Pharaoh is a bastard."

"Aaron, you mustn't talk like that," reproved his wife. "We are children of God. After all, every living person is descended from Adam and Eve. We're all one family — even Pharaoh."

"That I know," said Aaron, "I suppose, Pharaoh hails from YOUR side of the family!"

89

19. One day a clergyman and his wife were about to set off on their holiday. "Please don't pack your cassock," said his wife. "I am so tired of people, year after year, always knowing that you are a clergyman even when we are away on our holiday."

"All right," he said. He didn't pack it.

On their first day at the hotel, they had to share a table in the dining-room with a young couple.

"Excuse me," said the man, "I hope you don't mind my asking, but aren't you a clergyman?"

"Well, yes," replied the clergyman. "But how on earth did you know that I am a clergyman?"

"Well Sir," said the man, "your wife looks such a typical clergyman's wife."

18
FUND-RAISING

1. The Vicar had difficulty in collecting outstanding pew rents and he was only too pleased when his church warden offered to take over the job. The man was a rough diamond, but his heart was in the right place.

Sure enough, the money began to roll in, and the vicar was on the point of seeking out the warden to inquire how he had so swiftly succeeded, when he opened a letter that enlightened him.

It read: "Dear Vicar, Here is the money. I am sorry it was overlooked, but I would also take the opportunity of pointing out that my birth was quite legitimate and that 'lousy' is not spelt with a 'z'.

☆

2. A salesman was taking an evening off to sell tickets for church benefit. At one house the prospect said, "I'm sorry I have a very important engagement that evening so I won't be able to attend but I will be there with you in spirit."

"That's fine," said the quick-thinking salesman "Would your spirit like to sit in the 3 Dollar or 5 Dollar section?"

☆

3. The Pastorate Committee members of a Methodist Church were very busy trying to raise funds for a new project. It was tough going and money wasn't easy to get. Then one day the phone rang. It was a wealthy prostitute and she wanted to donate five thousand dollars for the project.

"Never," rasped the pastor. "We do not need that kind of money from the likes of you." A little later, she offered to donate ten thousand dollars. Once more she was rudely refused. Still a third time, the phone rang, and it was the same woman who offered the magnificent sum of twenty thousand dollars. This was more than the pastor could bear, so he called the Pastorate Committee for a conference.

"The contribution would put us over the top," he said, "but how can I take it from a woman who is running a brothel?"

At once the lay members of the Pastorate Committee sprang to their feet and cried out in one voice, "Don't be a fool, Pastor, Take it! After all, it is our money."

☆

4. Steven, a wealthy saloon keeper in Kensington, Philadelphia, was one of the main props of his church, but constant giving hurt a little. One day the priest came for a donation for new chimes for the steeple. Steven objected. "Who has come through with donations so far?" he asked.

The priest said, "I don't remember all the names. One gave 25 Dollars, one gave 50 Dollars, one gave 75 Dollars. You should give 100 Dollars, being the outstanding businessman of the community. You can afford it all right. Now you won't have any more to do about it. Just give me a cheque for 100 Dollars for these new chimes. They will sound beautiful in the neighbourhood, the chimes ringing."

"No, I think that's a little too much money," Steven said.

"Oh," the priest pleaded, "don't let me have to beg you for it."

Steven said, "Look, Father, about a week ago didn't you come through here asking a collection for the new steam heat for the church? I've got a wonderful idea that will save us a whole lot of money. Why don't you run a pipe up to the roof and put a whistle on it?"

☆

5. Once, while Bishop Talbot, the giant 'cowboy bishop', was attending a meeting of church dignitaries in St Paul's a tramp accosted a group of churchmen in the hotel porch and asked for aid.

"No," one of them told him, "I'm afraid we can't help you. But you see that big man over there?" pointing to Bishop Talbot. "Well, he is the youngest bishop of us all, and he's a very generous man. You might try him."

The tramp approached Bishop Talbot confidently. The others watched with interest. They saw a look of surprise come over the tramp's face. The bishop was talking eagerly. The tramp looked troubled. And then, finally, they saw something pass from one hand to the other. The tramp tried to slink past the group without speaking but one of them called to him: "Well, did you get something from our brother?"

"No," he admitted, "I gave him a dollar for his damned new cathedral at Laramie!"

☆

6. Then there was the congregation that was asked for money so often they insisted their pastor refer to them not as the flock but as the fleeced.

☆

7. Henry Ford, the automobile industrialist, was vacationing in Dublin. A delegation from a church orphanage came to his hotel room to request for a donation for a new building. Ford, without wasting any time, wrote out a cheque for £2,000.

The following day, a Dublin newspaper carried the front page headline: FORD GIVES £20,000 FOR IRISH ORPHANAGE." Later that morning the head of the orphanage came to Ford's suite to apologise and offered to phone the editor of the paper with a correction.

"That's all right," said the automobile tycoon, as he wrote out a cheque for £18,000. "You can have this cheque, but on one condition. When the new building opens, I want this inscription on it: "I WAS A STRANGER, AND YE TOOK ME IN."

☆

8. The crumbling, old church building needed re-modelling, so the preacher made an impassioned appeal, looking directly at the richest man in town.

At the end of the message, the rich man stood up and announced, "Pastor, I will contribute 1,000 Dollars."

Just then, plaster fell from the ceiling and struck the rich man on the shoulder. He promptly stood again and shouted, "Pastor, I will increase my donation to 5,000 Dollars."

Before he could sit back down, plaster fell, hitting him again, and again he virtually screamed, "Pastor, I will double my last pledge."

He sat down, and a larger chunk of plaster fell, hitting

him on the head. He stood once more and hollered, "Pastor, I will give 20,000 Dollars."

This prompted a deacon to shout, "Hit him again, Lord! Hit him again!"

☆

9. Bloggs, a lifelong resident of Minneapolis, was approached by a man asking him to help the Bible Society.

"Not I," exclaimed Bloggs. "I wouldn't give the Bible Society a dime, — you talk about St Paul all through the Bible — and not a word about Minneapolis."

☆

10. Three preachers were talking about what they would do if someone were to give them a million dollars. The first, a Methodist, said, "I should give half to foreign missions and half to home missions." The second said, "I would give some to foreign and home missions, but I would put some of it in the bank," He was a Presbyterian. The third, a Baptist, said, "We are not used to that kind of money, so I would first take it to a bank and ask if it were counterfeit. If it was good, then I would put it in my pocket and go to tell my deacons what to do."

19

LAUGHTER IN HEAVEN

1. To a person arriving in Heaven,
   Said St Peter, "We dine sharp at seven,
   Then breakfast's at eight —
   Never mind if you're late,
   And there's biscuits and milk at eleven."

☆

2. The Archangel Gabriel came to God, "There's a man to see you."

"Who is he?"

"He says his name's Epstein — claims to represent the Jewish people on earth."

"All right, show him in."

Epstein shuffled through the Pearly Gates. "Lord, the Jews are wondering if you could answer one question?"

"Certainly. Go on."

"Is it true that we are your Chosen People?"

"Yes."

"We are definitely your Chosen People?"

"Yes."

"Well Lord, the Jews are wondering if you could choose somebody else for a change."

☆

3. Paddy arrived at Heaven's gate. St Peter shook his head. "You're not on our list."

"To be sure," said Paddy. "I don't know why that should be, Sir."

"I am afraid I've been down all the O'Leary's and you are not here," said St Peter sorrowfully.

"Is there nothin' I can do then, your saintliness?" asked Paddy.

"It's too late now," replied the Apostle. "It's a question of what you've done in the past." Paddy looked crestfallen.

"Look," said St Peter, sympathetically, "perhaps I can put in a good word for you. Have you ever done anything very good, for instance?"

Paddy looked more depressed. His mind was even blanker than usual.

"All right," said the kindly saint, "What about something really brave, perhaps?"

"Oh well," said Paddy, brightening, "I did once stand in the middle of the Falls Road and shouted, "Down with all Catholics and Protestants."

"Remarkable," said St Peter. "When was that?"

"Oh, about thirty seconds ago."

☆

4. A wealthy man, noted during his life time for his selfishness and meanness, died and arrived outside the Pearly Gates. He was disconcerted to find that before entering he was required to explain why he should deserve admission. So he told St Peter that once on a cold winter's day, he had given two pence to an old lady who was starving, and on another occasion he had given a penny to a little boy whose parents had been killed in a revolution. St Peter transmitted this information to Gabriel and inquired, "What shall I do with this applicant?" and Gabriel said, "Give him his three pence back and tell him to go to hell."

☆

5. A man died and went to heaven. St Peter happened to have time on his hands and offered to show the new arrival round. As they walked from place to place, St Peter pointed to the different groups and explained who they were.

"They're the Jews... those over there are Buddhists... Those are Protestants... the ones in the corner are Mormons."

They arrived at a compound surrounded by a high wall. From inside could be heard the sound of voices and laughter.

"Who are those?" asked the new arrival.

"Hush!" said St Peter, "They're the Catholics — but they think they're the only ones here."

6. A story is told of a wealthy man who died and went to heaven and was interviewed by St Peter. At the conclusion St Peter reached out and pointed to a beautiful mansion nearby. "You may be interested to know that is your butler's home," he said.

"Well," the newcomer smiled in pleasant anticipation, "If that is his home, I can hardly wait to see what mine will be like."

Indicating a tiny cottage in the distance, St Peter murmured, "That hut over there is yours."

"But I can't live in that!" was the outraged answer.

"I am sorry, but you will have to," was the reply. "It's the best that I could do with the material you sent ahead while you were alive. We can only build here on the foundation you prepare while you are on earth."

☆

7. A Swiss delegation reports at the Pearly Gates and tells St Peter that they wish to see God. They are led to the presence of the Almighty and the leader of the delegation hands over a huge and altogether superb piece of cheese — a whole wheel of it. God asked what this is for. The leader explains: "This is the way the Swiss wish to express their gratitude to the creator for having made their country so beautiful, so wonderfully attractive and so prosperous. They also want to thank God for all tourists who make them rich."

God thanks them for their words. He expects them to leave but they do not move.

"Well," says God, "Is there anything else?"

"Yes, Almighty," replies the leader of the delegation, "the price of the cheese is 37 francs 50 centimes."

☆

8. A Protestant minister entered the Pearly Gates when his appointed time arrived, and was presented with a spanking new Chevrelet by St Peter. He went tooting all over Heaven in it contentedly, though he was a bit put out to observe Father Flanagan his old neighbour from the Catholic Church, whizzing by in a new model Buick convertible. When Rabbi Goldstein, however, drove up in a Cadillac limousine

97

with liveried chauffeur and footman, the Protestant was so annoyed he marched back to St Peter to register his protest. This is rank favouritism," he pointed out. "Why should I get just a Chevrelet and Rabbi Goldstein that snazzy Cadillac?"

"S-S-Sh," whispered St Peter. "You don't seem to understand. He is related to our boss."

☆

9. The Medici Pope, Pope Leo, organised the sale of indulgences on a vast scale, and this prompted Luther to publish his RESOLUTIONS. When Leo died, he went to heaven and knocked on the gate. St Peter called out and asked who it was.

"It's the Pope, open up."

But Peter was not satisfied. "If you are the Pope you should have the keys to heaven like all other Popes before you."

"I have the keys all right," replied Leo in plaintive voice. "But Luther has changed the lock."

☆

10. Joyce and Joey were killed in a plane crash the day before they were to have been married. St Peter welcomed them at the Celestial Gates and assured them that their heavenly stay would be a happy one.

"Thanks," said Joyce. "But you know we were killed the day before our marriage."

"Don't worry, my children," said St Peter. "I will see to it that you are married as soon as possible."

A month passed, then a year and 500 years passed. Then Joyce and Joey met St Peter and reminded him about his promise to get them married.

"I have not forgotten," said St Peter, "I am still waiting for a parson."

☆

11. The Pope and a lawyer, after their earthly stay, arrived at the Celestial Gates, and St Peter showed them their quarters. First the Pope was taken to his room, with a rickety chair, an old table and a Holy Bible. Then the lawyer was

taken to his room which was well furnished with all the luxuries.

"Excuse me," said the lawyer to St Peter, "there must be some mistake. Shouldn't the Holy Father have this room?"

"No. We have scores of Popes in Heaven, but you're our only lawyer."

☆

12. The souls of Roosevelt and Churchill fly up to Heaven. With true British pertinacity, Churchill arrives ahead of F.D.R. To his surprise he finds the Golden Gates closed and no sign of St Peter nearby. He cried alarmed to F.D.R., who is not far behind.

"Franklin! The Gates are closed!"

"Don't worry, Winston," cried F.D.R. "All you have to do is to break them down. I'll pay for them."

☆

13. Dan was eighty, and he wanted to have a good time before he died. He bought a hair piece, got silicone shots in his cheeks, had his double chin removed by plastic surgery, went to the gym to work out, and dressed up in mod clothes. He found a good looking widow of about forty and took her to ride in his brand new sports car. As he was escorting his date into a fancy restaurant, a bolt of lightning struck Dan. When he reached heaven, he cried, "Why me, God?" And God answered, "I'm sorry, Dan, I didn't recognise you."

☆

14. When President Franklin Delano Roosevelt died, he went to heaven where he was received by Moses. "Are you the Roosevelt that was fair and just President of the United States of America?"

"Yes," said Roosevelt.

"Ah, my son, Franklin, my heartfelt sympathies are with you for the scanty way the world treated your Four Freedoms," said Moses.

"Well, I think everything is relative," answered Roosevelt. "Your Ten Commandments aren't faring any better."

99

15. A man had been very sick and died in the hospital. When he arrived at the Pearly Gates, St Peter looked over his list and said, "We don't have your name on our list for today. Maybe you'd better try that other place."

"Oh, no," the man said. "I lived a good life. I went to church, was kind to people, donated to the poor, tried to live by the Golden Rule. Please, St Peter, don't turn me away. How about running my name through your computer again — maybe there's been a mistake."

So, St Peter ran his name through his giant computer and in a few minutes he had an answer for the waiting man.

"Yes," he said, "your name is here after all. But, you're not due here for another three years. Who was your doctor, anyway?"

20

LIMERICKS

1. There was a young fellow named Cain,
   Who was wicked, perverse, and profane;
      With the leg of a table
      He slugged brother Abel,
   And shouted, "Remember the Maine."

☆

2. The Reverend Henry Ward Beecher
   Called a hen a most elegant creature,
      Then the hen, pleased with that,
      Laid an egg in his hat.
   And thus did the hen reward Beecher.

☆

3. There once was a preacher named Blind,
   Who preached out of time and of mind.
      His hearers, alack,
      Got a pain in the back,
   And put pillows behind the behind.

☆

4. A hapless church tenor was Horace,
   Whose skin was so terribly porous,
      Some times in the choir
      He'd start to perspire,
   And nearly drown out whole chorus.

☆

5. A scrupulous priest of Kildare,
   Used to pay a rude peasant to swear,
      He would paint the air blue,
      For an hour or two,
   While his reverence wrestled in prayer.

☆

6. A modern young curate called Hyde,
   Will be pleased if the bishops decide

That, to govern a see,
One must hold a degree
In Evil, both pure and applied.

☆

7. There was an old person of Fratton,
Who would go to church with his hat on
"When I wake up," he said,
"With my hat on my head,
I shall know that it hasn't been sat on."

☆

8. The sermon our Pastor, — Rt. Rev.,
Began, may have had a rt. clev.,
But his talk, though consistent,
Kept the end so far distant,
That we left, as we felt he mt. nev.

☆

9. There was a young priest of Dun Laoghaire,
Who stood on his head in the KYRIE;
When people asked why,
He said in reply:
'It's the latest liturgical theory.'

☆

10. There was a pious young priest,
who lived almost wholly on yeast,
"For" he said, "it is plain
We must all rise again,
And I want to get started at least."

☆

11. There was a good Canon of Durham
Who fished with a hook and a worrum.
Said the Dean to the Bishop,
"I've brought a big fish up,
But I fear we will have to inter'm.

☆

12. There were two young ladies of Birmingham.
I know a sad story concerningham.

They stuck needles and pins
In the right reverend shins
Of the Bishop engaged in confirmingham.

13. A minister up in Vermont
Keeps a goldfish alive in his font;
    When he dips the babes in,
    It tickles the skin,
Which is all that the innocent want.

14. Goliath was known for ferocity,
An expert in every atrocity.
    But was knocked in a heap
    By a boy who kept sheep —
A victim of precocity.

15. There was once a parson from BUDE
Whose Manners at Table were rude,
    It wasn't the noise
    As he ate saveloy
But the way he sat on the food.

16. A soprano who sang in a choir,
Soared earnestly higher and higher,
    Till her uppermost note
    Got stuck in her throat
And lifted her clear through the spire.

17. Said a sceptical person of Lynn!
'I don't get this sharing of sin!
    'T would be awfully nice
    To annihilate vice,
But this is just spreading it thin!

18. There was a young chap with a kink,
Who boasted: 'I don't need to think

God-guided I am
Through the blood of Lamb,
Not to — mention the Oxford Group, Inc.,

☆

19. From a niche in the church of St Giles
Came a scream that resounded for miles.
"My goodness gracious,"
Said Brother Ignatius.
"How'd I know the bishop had piles."

21
MONKS AND NUNS

1. A Jesuit and a Benedictine were discussing their respective house-keepers. "Mine takes her recipe from the Old Testament," said the Benedictine sadly. "What do you mean?" asked the Jesuit, and the Benedictine replied, "They are either burnt offerings or bloody sacrifices."

☆

2. A Jesuit and a Benedictine were discussing their respective clothes. "God bequeathed us a comfortable habit of ample size," said the Benedictine, "whereas you wear tightly-fitting garments with those ridiculous wings at the back."

The Jesuit replied, "Surely it's better to have the wings than those habits."

☆

3. Two Benedictine monks were deep in conversation. Said the first, "Well, I'll give it to the Jesuits, they are fine educationists, splendid debators, and marvellous theologians and the Dominicans are superb intellectuals." The second nodded. "Quite right," he said, "and when it comes to humility, we are tops."

☆

4. Three monks of the Trappist Order, who live under a vow of silence, asked the abbot's permission to speak to one another. Permission was granted to the oldest monk to speak one sentence that year on a coming feast. The youngest of them was permitted to speak one sentence on the feast day one year later. The third brother was to wait still another year for his feast day privilege.

Following breakfast the first year, the oldest monk said, "I don't like porridge."

A year went by and after breakfast the youngest monk said, "I like porridge."

Another year passed and the third monk said, "I'm getting awfully tired of this constant squabbling over porridge."

5. A visitor in a monastery guest-house was awakened by an early knock on his door and the customary greeting: 'DOMINUS TECUM.'

"Thank you," he replied, "just put it down outside."

☆

6. A Jesuit and a Franciscan were dining together on a Friday. There were two pieces of fish on the table, one large and the other very small. The shrewd Jesuit helped himself to the large piece and put the small one on the Franciscan's plate.

"That certainly doesn't speak well of a Jesuit," said the Franciscan.

"Why?" asked the Jesuit in half jest.

The Franciscan said, "I have been trained in Holy Poverty. Had I served the fish, I should have put the large piece of fish on your plate and the small piece on mine."

"That's exactly what you got. Now, what are you complaining about?" said the Jesuit, without batting his eye-lid.

☆

7. A bare-footed and ill-clad Franciscan and a swollen-headed Dominican came to a ford at a stream. Seeing the swift-flowing stream and greatly mindful of his habit, the Dominican asked the Franciscan to carry him over to the other side of the stream. The Franciscan put him on his shoulders and carried him half-way, and then asked, whether he was carrying any money with him. "Only two reales," said the monk of the Dominican Order. But it was enough reason for the Franciscan to throw the Dominican into the stream. Then he said, "You know our strict rule. We are not allowed to carry money."

☆

8. King Charles the Bald of France had great respect for Notker, the monk for his virtue and learning. Once the king spent three days in the monk's monastery seeking his advice, both temporal and spiritual. When some nobles came to know about this they were jealous. So one of these jealous nobles planned to subject the monk to utter humiliation.

The monk was at his prayers in church when the jealous noble and his friends walked up to him and asked in a loud and rough voice, "We know you are a very learned man. Could you tell us what God is doing right now?"

Pat came the reply, "God is now exalting the humble and humbling the arrogant."

☆

9. In a monastery dedicated to prayer, Brother Gregory and Brother Alexander were discussing whether indulgence of the flesh could be permitted. They both had a weakness for cigarettes so they went to the abbot to ask his permission to smoke.

Brother Gregory went in and asked, "Is it all right to smoke while I am praying?"

The abbot slapped him across the face and ordered him to do forty days' penance. Brother Alexander went in and to the amazement of Brother Gregory — came out smiling.

"You mean, he didn't slap you and order you to do forty days' penance?"

"On the contrary," said Brother Alexander, "he congratulated me warmly! It's quite simple," said the artful monk. "You asked him whether it was all right to smoke while you were praying. I asked him whether it was all right to pray while I was smoking."

☆

10. The nun gave a long talk on sin, prayer, and forgiveness. When she had finished the lesson, she asked little Mary, "What do we have to do before we asked the Lord to forgive us?"

"Sin," replied Mary confidently.

☆

11. Sister Teresa was a saint with sharp wit and an inability to stand pomposity. "Self-importance was a balloon she pricked whenever she saw it bobbing along," is the way Phyllis Mcginley describes her in THE WIT OF SAINTS. A young nun came to her with exaggerated tales of temptations

107

she had to face and boasted of being a very great sinner.

"Now, sister," Teresa said deflatingly, "remember, none of us is perfect. Just make sure those sins of yours don't turn into bad habits."

☆

12. A rumour circulated that a nun in a convent was performing almost unbelievable miracles. The Pope sent St Philip of Neri to investigate. After a long journey, he finally reached the remote convent and asked to see the nun. As she entered the room, he pulled off his muddy boots and asked her to clean them. Haughtily the nun drew up her shoulders and scornfully turned away. St Philip put on his boots and returned to report to the Pope. He said, "His Holiness must give no credence to the rumours. Where there is no humility, there can be no miracles."

☆

13. A mother Superior, while travelling in a plane, was offered a cigarette by a fellow passenger.

The witty nun, as affable as ever, said, "No, thanks. One habit is enough for me."

☆

14. A Dominican, a Franciscan and a Jesuit were meeting in a room. In the middle of their discussion, the lights went out. Undeterred by the darkness, the Dominican stood up and said, "Let us consider the nature of light and of darkness, and their meaning."

The Franciscan began to sing a hymn in honour of "Our Little Sister Darkness."

The Jesuit went out and replaced the fuse.

☆

15. On the first day a Catholic sister wore the new contemporary dress adopted by her order, she noticed that the

boys in the maths class she taught were calmly surveying her legs. She turned to them and quipped, "Well, what did you expect? Wheels?"

☆

16. A nun applying for a passport, while going through the blank application form, paused right at the caption on the form—DISTINGUISHING MARKS. Then with a humorous twinkle in her eye, she wrote, "Nun."

☆

17. The Pope being convinced that complete abstinence from meat at mealtime was harmful to health of the monks of the Carthusian Order, ordered they be allowed to take meat. But their Father Superior sent the Pope a committee of twelve monks the youngest of whom was eighty years old, to urge the Supreme Pontiff to restore to vegetarianism. When the Holy Father saw these hale and healthy monks, he gently acquiesced.

☆

18. Sister Philomena and Sister Agnella went into a rural restaurant to have a quick lunch. While Sister Philomena was going through the menu carefully, the waiter stood closeby her respectfully, ready to take the orders from the nun. Finally, Sister Philomena said. "Will you please get me ham sandwich, waiter?"

The waiter said, "But today is Friday, Sister."

Sister Philomena sighed, "Oh, I am sorry! Bring me a cottage cheese then."

Sister Agnella looked up from her menu and eyes twinkling, said, "Is it still Friday?"

☆

19. The ebullient St Teresa of Avila abhorred unnecessary solemnity and pious pretentiousness. She prayed: "From silly devotions and sour-faced saints, good Lord, deliver us!"

St John of the Cross was her right hand in reforming the

Carmelite Order in Spain. He was a tiny man, not five feet tall. Teresa said of his size: "With John here, we have a monk and a half!"

When all her plans seemed failing and her reform impossible, she prayed to God in exasperation: "No wonder you have so few friends when you treat the ones you have so badly!"

22

PRAYERS

1. Life is fragile — handle it with prayer.

☆

2. Some people pray for a bushel but carry a cup.

☆

3. The following is the revised edition of an American prayer: "Forgive us our debts, O Lord, as we forgive our international debtors."

☆

4. An unreasonable prayer: "Lord, give this day our daily bread—with butter."

☆

5. Do not expect a thousand dollar answer to a ten-cent prayer.

☆

6. He who does not know how to pray when the sun shines will not know how to pray when the clouds come.

☆

7. A small boy prayed. "Lord, if you can't make me a better boy, don't worry about it. I'm having a good time as it is."

☆

8. Satan hinders prayers, but prayer also hinders Satan.

☆

9. "Kneeology" will do more for the world than theology.

☆

10. The prayer of modern youth seems to be: "Lord, lead us not into temptation. Just tell us where it is and we will find it."

11. Give me good digestion, Lord,
    And also something to digest:
    But where and how that something comes,
    I leave to Thee, who knoweth best.

☆

12. A CRICKETER'S PRAYER

Yorkshire and Lancashire were the great county sides. Emmot Robinson was Yorkshire's opening bowler and a useful batsman. One day the great rival teams were to play a decisive match in the competition so the great Emmot arrived very early. He looked in the Yorkshire dressing room and nobody was there. Then he grabbed a cushion and went into the shower room. He knelt on the cushion and prayed: "Dear Lord above, I know Thou art the greatest judge of any cricket match that ever takes place. Well, today, the two most powerful teams in county cricket oppose each other. Now, Lord, if Yorkshire have the best side they will win. And I suppose that if Lancashire have the best side, they will win. If the teams are equal or if it rains heavily, the game will be drawn. But Lord, if Thou wilt just keep out of it for the next seventy two hours, we'll knock the bloody hell out of this Lancashire lot."

☆

13. Abie was busy praying that he would win 10,000 on his premium bond. The first week winners were announced but there was nothing for Abie. Abie prayed harder than ever. "Please God, let me win a prize on the premium bond." The next week nothing happened.

Abie prayed and prayed,. "Let us win a prize."

But the next week, still nothing.

So Abie decided he was through with it all. "What's the good of praying," he asked God. Then God said, "Abie, meet me half way! At least buy a premium bond!"

☆

14. A little girl was moving with her family from Virginia to New York, and she was more than a trifle unhappy about it. The night before the family's departure she said her prayers, finishing off with usual, "God bless Mummy and Daddy, little brother Tommy, and everybody else." Then with

112

emphasis she added, "This is goodbye, God—we're moving to New York."

15. BICYCLIST'S PRAYER

Lord, Thou who never rodest a bicycle, help those who need it. Only Thou knowest the dangers we are subjected to and the difficulties we go through. Grant our prayer; help us on the upward slopes. There is no need to push us downwards. Support us when the brakes do not work. Support us, too, when the trouser leg gets caught in the metal chain. Deliver us from traffic Policeman, when we are on the wrong side of the street, in the few times we are on the right side. Remove from our path the stones (I am speaking of real stones) or we shall pass over them. Remove also the nails, the glass shards and other cutting and piercing objects. Sustain us, when we go through a deep hole full of water that seemed a shallow hole. Rescue us in the muddy streets, particularly when it is raining. Deflect us from the mud, when we are wearing clean clothes. Deliver us from bicycle thieves. Deliver us from dogs; those that like to run after us to bite the wheels. And, above all, help us to buy a car. Amen.
— Cleunice Orlandi de Lime

16. The new minister had asked Arthur to lead in prayer. It was Arthur's first experience of that kind of thing. Twenty minutes passed and he was still praying.

The congregation became restless. Finally, from one of the deacons came a strong "Amen." Arthur looked up and exclaimed, "Thanks." That's the word I've been trying to think of ever since I started."

17. The exactness of a Boston minister, a great precisionist in the use of words sometimes destroyed the force of what he was saying. On one occasion, in the course of an eloquent prayer, he pleaded:

"O Lord: waken thy cause in the hearts of this congregation and give them new eyes to see and new impulse to do. Send down Thy lev-or lee-ver, according to Webster's or

Worcestor's dictionary, whichever Thou usest, and pry them into activity."

☆

18. James McCosh, one-time President of Princeton University, New Jersey, USA, was leading chapel one morning when, during his closing prayers, he suddenly remembered an announcement he should have made. He realised that as soon as he pronounced the "Amen", the students would bolt for the doors, thus precluding any announcement. So, not deterred in the slightest, McCosh ended his prayer with these words: "And, Lord, bless the senior German Class, which meets this morning at 11 O'Clock instead of 10."

— *H. W. Corey.*

☆

19. One of the best stories Mark Twain told about himself was about the time when he was lecturing in a small American city and was being introduced by a local preacher. The good-hearted man began asking guidance and forgiveness for everyone present, naming them separately. Finally he wound up with: "Oh, Lord, we have with us a great American humorist. Help us to understand what he is about to say, and please, Lord, make us laugh as much as possible."

☆

20. PRAYER IN THE KITCHEN

This poem is said to have been written by a 19-year-old servant girl. It was read in a large congregation by Dr G. Cambell Morgan, at one of his last services in West Minster Chapel, London.

Lord of all pots and pans and things,
    Since I've no time to be
A saint by doing lovely things,
Or dreaming in the daylight, or
Strong Heaven's gates,
Make me a saint by getting meals and
Washing up plates.

Although I must have Martha's hand,
I have a Mary mind;

And then when I black the boots and shoes
Thy sandals, Lord, I find.
I think of how they trod the earth
What time I scrub the floor;
Accept this meditation, Lord,
I haven't time more.

Warm all the kitchen with Thy love, and
Light it with Thy peace.
Forgive me all my worrying, and make
All grumbling cease.
Thou who didst love to give men food
In room or by the sea,
Accept this service that I do —
I do unto Thee.

21. A PREACHER'S PRAYER

Dear Lord, fill my mind
With worth-while stuff—
And nudge me hard
When I've said enough.

22. SPEAKER'S PRAYER

"Lord, Thou knowest better than I know myself that I am growing older.

"Keep me from getting too talkative and on every occasion.

"Release me from craving to straighten out everybody's affairs.

"Teach me the glorious lesson that occasionally it is possible that I may be mistaken.

"Make me thoughtful, but not moody, helpful, but not bossy, Thou knowest, Lord, that what I want most is a few friends at the end."

☆

23. I am highly indebted to the Rt Rev Richard Harries, Bishop of Oxford for sending me this joke about a curate:-

A curate was late for church. Moreover, as he cycled the wind was hard against him so that he really had to struggle. When he arrived at the church nearly exhausted he realized he had left his sermon at home and would have to go back to fetch it. Thinking of the wind and in desperation, he prayed that God would help him by changing the direction of the wind!

☆

24. A newly-wed young lady went to a parish priest to seek his blessings. The priest laying his hand on her head, concluded his benediction as follows: "May God grant you a son at His earliest convenience!"

☆

25. A church deacon had done a bit of backsliding and had come home drunk the night before. Now, he was lying in bed suffering from an excruciating hangover.

His wife had tiptoed into the room and was trying to comfort him. "I think it would help if I said a prayer for you," she said.

He didn't say anything, so she began, "Lord, please help my husband. He is a good man. He feels so sick this morning because last night..."

At that point, the sick man opened his eyes and touched his wife on the hand. "Honey, please don't tell him I got drunk. Tell him I have the flu."

☆

26. A Presbyterian minister, the Rev Mr Houston, called on at short notice to officiate at the parish church of Crathie, attended by Queen Victoria, was so overcome with the importance of the occasion that he came out with the prayer: "Grant that as she grows to be an old woman, she may be made a man, and stand before Thee as a pure virgin, bringing forth sons and daughters to Thy glory; and in all peaceful causes she may go forth before people like a he-goat on the mountains." He was not asked to officiate again.

116

27. Father Taylor, an American R.C. priest, with a reputation for sincerity, once prayed: "O Lord, we ask Thee for a Governor who will rule in the fear of God; who will defeat the ringleaders of corruption, enhance the prosperity of the State, promote happiness of the people — O Lord, what's the use of beating about the bush. Give us George W. Briggs for Governor. Amen."

☆

28. A Methodist minister, on the last day of the Annual Conference, prayed: "Lord, be with the first speaker and give him power to inspire this people. And be with the second speaker and bless him with Thy spirit. And Lord, have mercy on the last speaker!"

☆

29. A minister, concerning a garrulous toastmaster, prayed: "Oh, Lord, from all traducers and introducers, deliver us!"

23
PULLING
THE LAYMAN'S LEG

1. It is said that when Henry VIII of England left the Church because the Pope would not annul his lawful marriage, the king had two priests summoned and said, "If you don't declare yourselves followers of Reformation, I will have you thrown into the Thames."

They replied, "All we want to do is to get to Heaven, and we don't care whether we get there by land or sea."

☆

2. When Bishop Phillips Brooks, author of "O Little Town of Bethlehem", was recovering from illness and not seeing any visitors, Robert Ingersoll, the anti-Christian propagandist, called to see him. He was admitted by the Bishop at once. "I appreciate this very much," said Ingersoll, "especially when you aren't permitting your close friends in to see you."

"Oh!" replied the Bishop, "I'm confident of seeing my friends in the next world but this may be my last chance of seeing you."

☆

3. An outdoor gospel service was in progress. A listener began to heckle the preacher. "Christianity hasn't done much good. It's been in the world for nineteen hundred years and look at the state of the world!"

Without batting an eyelash, back came the retort from the preacher, "And soap has been in the world longer than that and look at the dirt on your face!"

☆

4. A minister asked a man, "Why don't you go to church?"

Quick as a flash he answered, "The dying thief didn't join a church and he went to heaven."

"Have you been baptised?" the questioner continued.

"The dying thief never was."

"Do you give to missions?"

"No, the dying thief never did."

"Well," said the minister, "the only difference between you and that thief is that he was a dying thief and you are a living thief."

☆

5. Three priests dressed in the slacks and sports shirts were about to tee off when a golf hustler interrupted and asked if he could make up the foursome. "Okay," said the oldest priest, "but we must tell you — we are not good golfers."

Of course, the hustler swore, he too was a poor player. And how about a bet to make it more interesting? One of the priests protested they never bet, but to please him they made a rather steep wager.

Naturally, the golf-hustler won and the priests paid off. When they all returned to the locker rooms the hustler was shocked to see their habits and reluctantly offered to return the money.

"No," said the oldest priest, "we made a bet and we will stick to it — It will teach us a lesson."

"I still feel funny hustling priests," said the hustler. "Is there anything that I can do?"

"Do you have your parents?" asked the youngest priest.

"Yes, I do!"

"Well, bring them to me — and I'll marry them."

☆

6. Henry Ward Beecher sent the following note to the New York Ledger: "I have just received a curious letter from Michigan, and I give it to you verbatim.

"'Owasso City, Mich., 1970.

"'April Fool.'

"I have heard of men who wrote letters and forgot to sign their names, but never before met a case in which a man signed his name and forgot to write the letter."

☆

7. The telephone rang in the clergyman's office of the

Washington church which the President attended. An eager voice inquired, "Do you expect the President to be in church Sunday?"

"That," answered the clergyman, "I cannot promise. But we expect God to be there and we fancy that should be incentive enough for a reasonably large attendance."

☆

8. John Wesley, founder of Methodism, once confronted the dandy, Beau Nash, on a very narrow pavement in Oxford. Nash with an air of arrogance said, "I never make way for a fool."

"Don't you?" asked Wesley in half jest. "I always do." And he stepped aside.

☆

9. Canon Sydney Smith, the famous English wit, was as usual getting the best of the argument with a lawyer friend of his. The lawyer, who had an exaggerated estimate of his debating skill, could not stand losing and in disgust snapped ill-humouredly, "If I had a son who was an idiot, I would make him a parson."

Canon Smith shot back, "Your father was obviously of a different opinion."

☆

10. Once while addressing an open-air meeting, an agnostic asked a bishop if he believed that Jonah was swallowed by a whale.

"When I go to heaven, I will ask Jonah," said the prelate.

"But suppose you won't find him there?" the agnostic asked.

"Then you will have to ask him," was the quick reply.

☆

11. Henry Ward Beecher was as good as Sydney Smith in making friends with all faiths. Riding in a horse-drawn carriage, some boorish fellows were scoffing at religion and making uncouth reference to his priestly attire.

As Rev Beecher left the carriage, he spoke to the juvenile

delinquents, for the first time, "We shall meet again."

One of the boys asked impolitely, "Where?"

"You know," said Beecher, "I am the visiting chaplain in several prisons in this district."

☆

12. Once John Wesley shared a carriage with an army officer who though was a fine conversationist, couldn't help using swear words. The founder of Methodism was somewhat piqued by the officer's language, but was tactful enough not to show his resentment.

When they stopped to change the coach horses, Wesley said to him, "May I ask you a favour?"

The army officer said, "Yes." The great evangelist said, "We will be travelling some distance together. And if I should forget myself and use swear words, in front of the ladies, kindly correct me."

The officer immediately took the hint and Wesley's method of rebuke worked perfectly.

☆

13. A pastor phoned the municipal office to ask that a dead mule be removed from the front of the church. The young clerk, who took the phone, thought he would be smart. "I thought you clergymen took care of the dead," he remarked flippantly.

"We do," answered the pastor, "but first we get in touch with their relatives."

☆

14. A young priest was travelling in a train from Rome to Naples. His fellow passengers were three newly-converted communists from a factory in Rome. Noticing his clerical garb and his long gray beard, the commies began to make fun of him. But the elderly priest paid scant regard to their taunts. Then the reds had some other idea. Each of them addressed the priest in turn:

"Good morning, father Abraham!"
"Good morning, father Isaac!"
"Good morning, father Jacob!"

It was more than the priest could bear. "You are mistaken, my good friends," replied the priest. "I am not any of the patriarchs. I happen to be Saul, whose father sent him out in search of the lost asses. I thank God that I have found them much sooner than I had anticipated."

15. A Durham miner approached the Bishop in a spirit of levity, and explained that he was anxious about the future life. What worried him was how he would manage to get his wings inside his waistcoat. "That, my dear fellow," said the Bishop blandly, "is not a problem that need worry you. Your difficulty will be to get your tail inside your trousers."

24
QUESTIONS & ANSWERS

1. What is the difference between a church bell and a pickpocket?

One peals from the steeple and the other steals from the people.

☆

2. Who was the most popular actor in the Bible?
Samson. He brought down the house.

☆

3. In Biblical times what did people use to do arithmetic?
The Lord told them to multiply on the face of the earth.

☆

4. When was medicine first mentioned in the Bible?
When the Lord gave Moses two tablets.

☆

5. When would it be wrong to cut off a cat's tail?
The Bible says, "What God hath joined together let no man put asunder."

☆

6. Who are heathens?
Heathens are people who don't quarrel over religion.

☆

7. What are the sins of omission?
They are the sins we should have committed but didn't.

☆

8. Why was Noah the first businessman mentioned in the Bible?

Because he floated a company at a time when the rest of the world was under liquidation.

☆

9. Why is a church like a convention?
Because families send just one delegate.

☆

10. Why are the Ten Commandments so brief?
They didn't come through a committee.

☆

11. Does your church have a big gun?
No, but our cathedral does have a canon.

☆

12. What books, apart from the Bible, have helped you most?
My mother's cookbook and my father's chequebook.

☆

13. What is the first message, should the missionaries teach the cannibals?
To be vegetarians.

☆

14. Why do people fall asleep in church?
The longer the spoke, the greater the tire.

☆

15. Skeptic (discussing Balaam's steed): How is it possible for an ass to talk like a man?
Parson: Well, I don't see why it ain't as easy for an ass to talk like a man as it is easy for a man to talk like an ass.

☆

16. Isn't it scandalous? The minister's son has decided to become a jockey? He was to have been a minister, you know. Well, don't worry. He'll bring a lot more people to repentance than he would as a minister.

17. Why did the Puritans leave England for America?

So that they could carry on their religion in freedom and in their way force others to do likewise.

☆

18. What did Noah do in the dark?
He switched on the floodlights.

☆

19. Why is that some young men enter ministry?

Because it is easier to stand up and yell than to sit down and listen.

☆

20. What's the difference between a church and a movie theatre? In church they "Pray in the name of Jesus". In a theatre they say, "Shut up for Christ's sake."

☆

21. Why is it easier to be a clergyman than a physician?
Because it is easier to preach than to practise.

☆

22. Why was Adam a famous runner?
Because in the human race he was first.

☆

23. When Adam and Eve left the Garden of Eden what did they do?
They raised Cain.

☆

24. Why didn't they play cards on Noah's Ark?
Because Noah sat on the deck.

☆

25. What is the difference between a Christian and a Cannibal? The one enjoys himself, and other enjoys other people.

26. At what season did Eve eat the apple?
Early in the fall.

☆

27. At what time of day was Adam created?
A little before Eve.

☆

28. Why was Pharaoh's daughter like a broker?
Because she got a little prophet from the rushes on the
bank.

25
QUIPS & QUOTES

1. The atheist can't find God for the same reason that a thief can't a policeman.

☆

2. An atheist hopes the Lord will do nothing to disturb his disbelief.

☆

3. The worst possible moment for an atheist is when he feels grateful and has no one to thank.

☆

4. If there are any good traits about the atheist, he got them from Christianity.

☆

5. An empty tomb proves Christianity; an empty church denies it.

☆

6. Satan is perfectly willing to have a person profess Christianity as long as he does not practise it.

☆

7. Christianity helps us face the music, even when we don't like the tune.

☆

8. Some people can talk Christianity by the yard but they can't or won't walk it by the inch.

☆

9. When tempers grow hot, Christianity grows cold.

☆

10. The greatest service that could be rendered the Christian people would be to convert them to Christianity.

11. Christians are the light of the world, but the switch must be turned on.

☆

12. A Christian shows what he is by what he does with what he has.

☆

13. If people have to ask you if you're a Christian, you're probably not.

☆

14. Every Christian occupies some kind of pulpit and preaches some kind of sermon every day.

☆

15. What most Christians need is fewer platitudes and better attitudes.

☆

16. What the world needs is not more Christianity but more Christians who practise Christianity.

☆

17. There are some Christians who can't be called 'Pilgrims' because they never make any progress.

☆

18. The Christian should learn two things about his tongue — how to hold it and how to use it.

☆

19. Beware of a Christian with an open mouth and a closed pocketbook.

☆

20. When Christians feel safe and comfortable, the church is in its greatest danger.

☆

21. Some Christians have will power, others have *won't* power.

22. The Christian life is like an airplane — when you stop, you drop.

☆

23. Many churches are plagued with a lot of 'retired' Christians.

☆

24. The weekend religion of some Christians is weak at both ends, and unreliable between the two ends.

☆

25. The Lord prepares a table for His children, but too many of them are on a diet.

☆

26. Nowadays, we have sermonettes by preacherettes for Christianettes.

☆

27. Some people seem willing to do anything to become a Christian except to give up their sins.

☆

28. Many church services are today marked by lameness, tameness and sameness.

☆

29. Not many people are attracted to churches which are as cold as ice or by preachers who are as dry as dust.

☆

30. The business of the Church is to get rid of evil, not to supervise it.

☆

31. The great task of the Church is not only to get sinners into heaven, but to get saints out of bed.

☆

32. Too many Churches have become distribution centres for religious aspirins.

33. The Church is a building and loan association to help you build a mansion in heaven.

☆

34. The Church is paralysed with timidity and gradually dying of dignity.

☆

35. The world at its worst needs the Church at its best.

☆

36. Blessed is the man who can hear his alarm clock on Sunday as well as on Monday.

☆

37. It seems some refuse to come to the front of the church unless escorted by pallbearers.

☆

38. Judging by church attendance, heaven won't be crowded with men.

☆

39. Some folk's church going is like ice-cream — it disappears when the weather gets hot.

☆

40. Blessed is the man whose watch keeps church time as well as business time.

☆

41. There are four classes of church members: the tired, the retired, the tiresome and the tireless.

☆

42. A sickly saint is likely to be a healthy hypocrite.

☆

43. It is far better to be a weak church member than to be a strong sinner.

44. There are still a few church members like the farmer's pond — dried up in the summer and frozen in the winter.

☆

45. A lot of church members know the twenty-third psalm much better than the Shepherd.

☆

46. It seems church members have been starched and ironed, but not washed.

☆

47. Many churches have three kinds of members — pickers, kickers and stickers.

☆

48. There are a few church members who may be described as the farmer described his mule: "Awfully backward about going forward."

☆

49. God gives us the ingredients for our daily bread, but he expects us to do the baking.

☆

50. If you are disgusted and upset with your children, just imagine how God must feel about His.

☆

51. Don't cheat the Lord and call it economy.

☆

52. God doesn't expect us to solve all the world's problems — He expects us not to create them.

☆

53. The first thing the typical American will ask when he gets to heaven is the amount of the down-payment on a harp.

☆

54. Our Lord does not open the windows of heaven to the person who keeps his Bible shut.

55. When you get to heaven you will be surprised to see many people there you do not expect to see. Many may be just as surprised to see you there.

☆

56. Almost everybody is in favour of going to heaven, but many people are hoping they'll live long enough to see easing of the entrance requirements.

☆

57. Some people want to go to heaven for the same reason they want to go to California — they have relatives there.

☆

58. Judging from the way some people behave these days, they must be thinking that hell is air-conditioned.

☆

59. There is a way to stay out of hell, but no way to get out.

☆

60. Since the old-time evangelist has almost disappeared from the scene, hell doesn't seem half as hot as it used to be.

☆

61. No matter how many translations of the Bible are made, the people still sin the same way.

☆

62. The wages of sin are the only wages not subject to the income-tax.

☆

63. Our Government could raise unlimited revenue simply by taxing sin.

☆

64. A preacher who will not try to practise what he preaches is not fit to be listened to.

65. When some preachers get up, their thoughts sit down.

☆

66. All preachers should be sure of what they are saying. Someone in the audience might be listening.

☆

67. If a preacher can't strike oil in thirty minutes, it shows he's either using a dull auger or he's boring in the wrong place.

☆

68. A preacher in Alabama was fired for two reasons. First, he had a poor delivery. Second, he never had very much to deliver.

☆

69. Preachers should learn that for a sermon to be immortal it need not be eternal.

☆

70. Many tailor their religion to fit the pattern of their prejudice.

☆

71. In our generation the popular religion is CONFU-SIONISM.

☆

72. You cannot prove your religion by its noise.

☆

73. We are more comfortable with Christ in print than in practice.

☆

74. Some folks seem to think religion is like a parachute — something to grab when an emergency occurs.

☆

75. Isn't it strange how some people insist on having expensive clothes, yet are perfectly satisfied with a shoddy religion?

76. Most people have some sort of religion; at least they know what church they're staying away from.

☆

77. The religion of some is well-developed at the mouth but lame in the hands and feet.

☆

78. When your religion gets into past tense, it becomes pretense.

☆

79. The devil also loves a cheerful giver provided he is the receiver.

☆

80. Old Satan has no unemployment problems.

☆

81. Satan uses a vacant mind as a dumping ground.

☆

82. Satan doesn't care what we worship as long as we don't worship God.

☆

83. No bald-headed man was ever converted by a sermon during the fly season.

☆

84. Every sermon should change the person in the pew, or it should be changed by the preacher in the pulpit.

☆

85. The eternal gospel does not require an everlasting sermon.

☆

86. You can read the world's shortest sermon on a traffic sign: "Keep right."

87. Scratch the Christian you find the pagan.

☆

88. In all ages hypocrites called priests have put crowns upon the thieves called kings.

☆

89. The Puritans hated bear-baiting not because it gave pain to the bear but it gave pleasure to the spectators.

☆

90. To a philosophic eye, the vices of the clergy are far less dangerous than their virtues.

☆

91. A Christian is a man who feels repentance on Sunday for what he did on Saturday and what he is going to do on Monday.

☆

92. Better go to heaven in rags than to hell in embroidery.

☆

93. A house-going parson makes a church-going people.

☆

94. Take heed before an ox, of a horse behind, of a preacher on all.

☆

95. The devil gets up to the belfry by the vicar's skirt.

☆

96. A man is accepted into the church for what he believes and he is turned out for what he knows.

☆

97. The main business of a Christian soul is to go through the world turning water into wine.

98. Some Christians are like the candles that have been lit once and then put away in a cupboard to be eaten up by mice.

☆

99. Nowadays, the world is full of tame Christians; in consequence, the churches are empty of life, if not of people.

☆

100. Churches in cities are the most wonderful solitudes.

☆

101. It is not well for a man to pray cream and live skim-milk.

☆

102. The best sermon has a good beginning and a good ending and not too much space between them.

26
RELIGIOUS PUNS

1. A church fair is a bazaar experience.

☆

2. The priest jogged round the graveyard in order to exercise the spirit.

☆

3. A Puritan is a man who 'noes' what he likes.

☆

4. The Mother Superior says that if I don't study harder, I'll be in this convent for reverend ever.

☆

5. The minister of one particular small church was his own book-keeper. His bills were neatly filed away in a box marked, 'Due unto others.'

☆

6. The rural vicar decided that he would try to raise chickens in order to supplement his income. Each morning, he went out into the garden to see if the eggs he had bought had hatched. Finally, one morning, he found they all had, and there were dozens of fluffy little chicks. "Ah," he murmured thankfully, "my coop runneth over."

☆

7. When the bishop was at the barber's one day, he became aware of rather a strange odour. "What's that strange smell?" he demanded. "Oh," said his barber, "forgive me, father, for I have singed."

☆

8. The three Wise Men each carried only one gift because they had believed in travelling light.

9. The reason the old church in our village has irregular recesses in its walls is that the builder lost the plans. In consequence the edifice suffers from an apse of memory.

☆

10. The Tower of Babel was the din of iniquity.

☆

11. I always thought that Wolseley was a cardinal car.

☆

12. When the Great Flood had abated, Noah sent the animals off the Ark, enjoining each couple to 'go forth and multiply'. As he was clearing up afterwards, he came upon two snakes. 'I thought I told you to go forth and multiply,' he exclaimed. "We are sorry, Sir, but we can't," one of them replied. "You see, sir, we are adders."

☆

13. When hard times came upon the monastery, the abbot decided to set up a fish and chip shop at the entrance. Brother Jonathan was put in charge of frying the fish, and Brother Leonard was put in charge of the spuds. The local citizens soon learned to ask for one man or the other when they wanted just fish or just chips. One night, a newcomer to the area went in. He wanted just fish, and said to the man behind the counter, "I say, are you the fish friar?" "No," said Brother Leonard, "I'm the chip monk."

☆

14. When Eve tried to get out of the garden without him, Adam called up to the Commanding Officer, "Eve is absent without leaf!".

☆

15. Needless to say, the Vatican isn't inclined to believe infidel Castro.

☆

16. Samson loved Delilah, until she bald him out.

138

17. Beware of Satan or evil have his way.

☆

18. As St Peter says to every new arrival as they approach the Pearly Gates "Well, halo there."

☆

19. **AN ANSWER TO THE PARSON**
"Why of the sheep do you not learn peace?"
"Because I don't want you to shear my fleece."

☆

20. An indolent vicar of Bray,
His roses allowed to decay,
His wife, more alert,
Bought a powerful sqirt
And said to her spouse, "Let us spray."

21. A guest Baptist preacher was being introduced to a large Presbyterian gathering. Said the Chairman, "Our guest speaker had trouble with his speech when he was young. A speech therapist told him to put five marbles in his mouth in the morning and speak all day that way. Then next day, three, next two. Then one. "Then," he said, "When you have lost all your marbles, you will become a Baptist preacher." When the preacher rose, he commented, "That was marbelous introduction!"

☆

22. Our church was looking for a new clergyman and the selection committee finally recommended a young man just out of the seminary. Many older church members protested that a more experienced man would have been preferable. Committee members retaliated with the argument that a younger man might breathe fresh life into the congregation.

At the end of the meeting, I commented to an older man that this marked the beginning of better things for our church. "Yes," he said with a wry smile, "move on to greener pastors."

Jerry Riggs

139

23. The pastor's morning prayer began, "O Lord, give us clean hearts, give us pure hearts, give us sweet hearts," and every girl in the congregation fervently responded, "Ah-men!"

☆

24. A man was painting the church building. Noticing that he would not have enough paint to finish, he added thinner. As the paint continued to run out the painter added more and more thinner.

A rainstorm the next day washed away his paint job. The pastor met the painter on the job and demanded that he "repaint and thin no more."

☆

25. A Catholic priest and a Methodist Minister were driving rather rapidly down a country road headed to the golf course. The priest ran over a rabbit that was playing in the road. He stopped the car, took a vial out of the glove compartment, and said to his companion; "I am really very sorry I did that. At least I can give the poor creature the last rites." Whereupon he anointed the prone rabbit with holy water.

The Methodist then took a bottle out of his golf bag and sprinkled some of its contents on the apparently lifeless bunny. Immediately the rabbit came to life, jumped into the air, and in a moment had run across a nearby field.

The priest was astonished. "I didn't know you Methodists used such potent holy water," he remarked. "We don't," replied the minister. "That was a hare restorer."

☆

26. Farmer Hiram had a fairly big poultry farm. He kept a careful check on the laying of his hens, and those that were poor layers, quickly found their way into the oven. One day the village parson who was known for his devastating punning, was invited to dinner. When his plate was heaped high with roast chicken, he remarked, "Here's where the chicken enters the ministry."

"I hope," rejoined Farmer Hiram, who was also a past-master at punning himself, "that it does better there than it did in lay work."

27. A cannibal complained to a colleague that he suffered a bad case of indigestion after eating a Franciscan missionary. "How did you cook him?" asked second cannibal.

"I boiled him."

"That was your mistake. You should never boil Franciscans. They are friars."

☆

28. A student from a Bible college vacationing at his home, one day went to his farm to run a bulldozer. He sat at the supper table meddling with a rip in his favourite jeans, where his mending job had failed to hold.

With wisdom gained from three years of dorm life in the Bible college and three hundred miles away from home, he concluded solemnly, "Whatsoever a man seweth, that shall he also rip."

141

27

SAYING GRACE

1. Heavenly Father, bless us,
    And keep us all alive.
    There's 10 of us for dinner,
    And enough for five. — Amen.

☆

2. Charles Lamb was in the habit of wearing a white cravat, and in consequence was sometimes taken for a clergyman. Once at a dinner table, among a large number of guests, his white cravat caused such a mistake to be made, and he was called on to 'say grace'. Looking up and down the table, he asked in his inimitable lisping manner: "Is there no cl-cl clergyman present?"

"No, Sir," answered a guest.

"Then," said Lamb, bowing his head, "let us thank God."

☆

3. Lady Edwina Mountbatten was training a new maid. "Now, Emma," she said, "I am expecting a friend to tea, the Duchess of So-and-So. I wish you to tell her that I will be a few minutes late. Ask her to wait for me and show her into the drawing room. And don't forget to say 'Your Grace'."

When the Duchess arrived, the maid delivered her little speech all right. And with Lady Mountbatten's last instruction to say 'Your Grace', ringing in her ears, she made a little curtsy, saying "And may the Lord make us truly thankful."

☆

4. A parson's wife was very particular about saying grace before meals, even if the dinner consisted entirely of leftovers. One night the parson had a look at the stale food with aversion and started eating in silence.

"My dear," reproved his wife mildly, "how is that you have forgotten to say grace?"

"When every scrap of edible food has been blessed three

times," said the parson sharply, "what difference does it make if I don't say grace."

☆

5. Benjamin Franklin, as a child, found the long graces by his father before and after meals, very annoying. One day, when his father was salting down the winter's provisions, the little Ben said, "I think, Daddy, if you were to say grace over the whole cask once for all, it would be a vast saving of time and botheration."

☆

6. The Baptist minister was in the habit of saying very long graces before meals. One evening, while he was saying grace, his little son piped up from the corner of the table, "Daddy," chirped the little son, "why didn't you say 'et cetera' like you are telling me?"

"My son," chided the father sternly, "I wasn't talking to you."

☆

7. Mona had been rude to her parents and the punishment meted out to her was that she eat her dinner alone at a small table in a corner of the kitchen. No one cared to pay any attention to her until the family heard the grace she was saying aloud, "I thank Thee Lord, for preparing a table for me in the presence of my enemies."

☆

8. A rural pastor was noted for his brevity of words when he said grace at meals. When he was invited to a lavish meal, he said, "Bountiful Jehovah, we present our thanks to Thee for Thy abundant providences." But at a simple meal, he would say, "Lord, teach us to thank you for the least of Thy mercies."

☆

9. The Sunday School teacher, after teaching her pupils the importance of saying grace before meals, turned to a boy, whose father was an Elder and a pillar of the Church, and said,

"Now, Johnny, what is the first thing your father says, when he comes to the dining table?"

To her dismay Johnny said, "He says, Go easy on the butter, children, it's two dollars a pound."

☆

10. Mrs Imelda de Silva once invited a newly-appointed priest to have dinner with her family. She asked the priest to lead them in saying Grace. When the priest concluded saying Grace, her five-year daughter, Evelyn seemed to be highly excited. After dinner, when all had risen from the table Evelyn rushed over, drew her mother inside, and said in a whisper, "Mom! He knows my friend, Grace."

☆

11. Mr Justice Swift was invited to the Bar mess at Exeter when he was on circuit. Du Parcq, as senior silk that night, presided and had the duty of saying the two-word grace. 'Benedictus benedicat', before dinner, 'Benedicto benedicatus' after.

"My dear Parcq," said the judge, "do you think that the Almighty will be angry with me if I don't stand up while you say grace?"

"Oh, no Judge, I don't think so," was the reply, "he'll just think you don't understand Latin."

☆

12. Little Monty, son of a radio announcer, when called upon to say grace at a family dinner, bowed his head and said in a loud clear voice, "This food comes to us through the courtesy of Almighty God."

☆

13. Betty, four, out to dinner, was a bit surprised when she saw the hosts bow their heads for grace.

"What are you doing?" she asked.

"Giving thanks for our daily bread," she was told. "Don't you give thanks at home, Betty?"

"No," said Betty, "we pay for our food."

14. Jerome, a businessman, asked to say grace and being unaccustomed to the ceremony, said, "Dear Lord, we are in receipt of your kind favour of recent date and beg to thank you. We hope to merit continued courtesy."

☆

15. Just as Harry A. Ironside was about to begin his meal in a crowded restaurant, a man approached and asked if he could join him. Then, as was his custom, Ironside bowed his head in prayer.

When he opened his eyes, the other man asked, "Do you have a headache?" Ironside replied, "No, I don't." The other man asked, "Well, is there something wrong with your food?" Ironside responded, "No, why?" "Well," the man said, "I saw you sitting there with your head down and I thought you must be sick, or that there was something wrong with your food." Ironside replied, "No, I was simply thanking God as I always do before I eat." The man said, "Oh, you're one of those, are you? Well, I want you to know I never give thanks. I earn my money by the sweat of my brow and I don't have to give thanks to anybody when I eat. I just start right in!" Ironside said, "Yes, you're just like my dog. That's what he does too!"

28
SERMONS IN SMILES

1. As a pastor was to begin his Sunday sermon on a sultry morning, an usher opened the windows near the front for cross-ventilation. A sudden gust of wind blew his notes out of the window and out of the sight.

"Folks," said the pastor, "I did have a message for you. Now I guess I'll have to trust the Lord."

☆

2. A man preached and preached. First, people began to walk out one by one, then two's, as husbands and wives departed. The whole families went out. Finally, only one man remained, staying right to the end. "Pardon me, Sir," asked the speaker, "but I have noticed you have stayed to the end and I would like to ask you why."

Came the reply, "Because I am the next speaker."

☆

3. When Henry Ward Beecher was minister of Plymouth Church, Brooklyn, his brother agreed to fill the pulpit one Sunday. The house was packed, but when it was noticed that the regular minister would not preach, a number arose to leave.

'Father Tom', as the other preacher was known, announced, "All who came to worship Henry Ward Beecher this morning may depart at this time. The rest will stay to worship God." The exodus ceased.

☆

4. A sexton dusting the pulpit after Sunday service took a quick look at the pastor's manuscript. Along the left margin, he read these instructions, 'pause here,' 'wipe eyebrow', 'use angry fist here,' 'look upward'. Near the end was a long paragraph of texts, opposite which the pastor had marked in block letters: 'ARGUMENT WEAK HERE, YELL LIKE HELL.'

5. It was raining cats and dogs, and the preacher preached and preached. Realising that he had kept the audience too long in their seats, he said, "I'm afraid, I have kept you too long."

Whereupon a voice from the backbench said, "No, go right on, pastor, it's still raining."

☆

6. The parson, who was known for his verbal high gear, preached beyond the span of attention of the audience. The parson, hurt by the lack of interest in his sermon pointedly reproved the congregants thus: "I do not mind your looking at your watches from time to time, but when you hold them to your ears and shake them to determine if they are still running, that's going a trifle too far."

☆

7. The Bishop Graf Galan is giving a sermon in the Cathedral in which he is preaching the education of young people in the Hitler Jugend. Someone shouts from the crowded congregation: "How can a man who has no children dare to preach about the education of children?"

To which Galan replies, "I cannot allow such personal criticism of the Fuhrer in my church."

☆

8. There was the pot-bellied minister who had a problem keeping his shirt properly tucked into his trousers. He was very sensitive about this and was always stuffing it back. One day he was invited to speak at another church. During the sermon he ran his hand around the back of his trousers and sure enough there was the excess material. He started stuffing and by the time he finished preaching, he had discovered to the glee of the audience that he had stuffed more than half of the national flag into his trousers.

☆

9. A Negro preacher began his sermon by saying, "Brethren, and sisters, here you is coming to pray for rain. I'd like to ask you just one question — where is yo' umbrellas?"

10. The young pastor's first sermon held the audience speechless! He challenged them to gird their loins for Christian service and living. To their consternation, he preached the same sermon the following Sunday. When he inflicted upon them the same ringing message, the congregants thought something must be done.

"Don't you have more than just one sermon, parson?" asked an Elder.

"Oh, yes," he replied quickly, "I have quite a lot of sermons. But you haven't done anything about the first one yet."

☆

11. A travelling preacher, after the sermon in a country church, was asked by a parishioner why God sends epidemics into the world.

The preacher replied, "Some times folks get so bad that they must be removed and therefore the coming of the epidemics is justified."

"But," objected the parishioner, "how come that so many good people get removed with the bad ones?"

"The good ones are summoned for witnesses," he explained. "The good Lord aims to give everyman a fair trial."

☆

12. SERMON SAMPLER

COTTON CANDY SERMON
Very sweet and full of air;
When bitten into, nothing there.

STUFFED OLIVE SERMON
Pleasantly fashioned, pleasingly tart,
Stuffed with intellect but no heart.

JELLO FRUIT SALAD SERMON
Shaking, prancing, quivering preaching,
Lots of action but low calorie teaching.

POACHED EGG SERMON
Soft, safe, sentimental food,
Soothes every mind, calms every mood.

148

LEFTOVER TURKEY SERMON
Meat they suspect you've served them before,
But disguised enough for one Sunday more.

HOT TAMALE SERMON
Full of fire, not hard-shell,
Pious hate, threatening hell.

STRAWBERRY AND WHIPPED CREAM SERMON
Summer surprise, memorable, bright,
Light in weight but what a delight.

ROAST BEEF AND POTATOES SERMON
Familiar fare but always good,
The gospel preached in words understood.

☆

13. "How did you like my sermon yesterday, Mr Sydney?" asked the young pastor of a small rural church.

"Well," was the thoughtful reply, "I don't really get a fair chance at your sermon. I'm an old man now, and I have to sit in the backbenches! And there is Mrs Franklin, and widow Flynn, and Mrs Johnson and her children, and all the rest of them sitting in front row, with their mouths wide open, swallowing down all the best of the sermon, and — well, what gets down to me is pretty poor stuff, parson, pretty poor stuff."

☆

14. There was a long-winded minister who preached from Genesis to Revelation in every sermon. One day, after having covered almost the whole of the Bible, he said, "Now we have come to Isaiah — what shall we do with him?"

One old man said, "He can have my seat, brother, I am leaving."

☆

15. Wilcox walked into the railroad station and said to the man in-charge, "I want you to give orders to the engineer of the express to stop blowing the whistle on Sunday mornings."

"That ain't possible," said the official. "Why do you want to do that for?"

"Well, our parson preaches until he hears the train

149

whistle blow — and that confounded express was thirty-five minutes late last Sunday."

☆

16. President Calvin Coolidge was once asked after a Sunday morning church service, what the preacher's subject had been. The President replied, "He preached on sin."

"What did the preacher say about sin?" the questioner continued.

Coolidge replied, "He was against it."

☆

17. It had been many a month since he had been to church, but his wife who was a regular church-goer, had induced him to go to church one Sunday morning. He volunteered to stand at the entrance of the church and greet people as they entered. Everything went smoothly and he was highly elated to find himself greeting the people. Soon he welcomed a latecomer with the usual, "Good morning, glad to see you here today."

"Oh, I try to be here as often as I can," said the latecomer gently and then proceeded to the pulpit and started the service.

☆

18. The Rev DeLamotta, chaplain at Paine College, Augusta, preached the shortest sermon in the college's 80-year history. His topic was, "What Does Christ Answer When We Ask: 'Lord, What's In Religion For Me?"

The complete text of his remarks: "Nothing."

He said later that his sermon was a corrective for people 'brought up on the gimme-gimme gospel'.

Asked how long it had taken to prepare his message, Dr DeLamotta replied, "Twenty years."

☆

19. The recently appointed bishop to the court of Queen Victoria was very keen to make a grand impression with his first sermon, and asked Benjamin Disraeli for his advice. "How long, Mr Prime Minister, do you think, my sermon should last?" he inquired.

"A most perplexing question to answer," replied Disraeli. "Generally, I should say that if you preach for forty minutes, Her Majesty will be satisfied; for thirty minutes, she will be delighted; if you preach for only fifteen minutes — Her Majesty will be enthusiastic."

☆

20. One famous preacher asked for his formula for a successful sermon, answered: "Begin slow, go slow, rise higher, take fire, and sit in the storm."

☆

21. Bishop M. Elia Peter who is known for his subtle wit and gentle humour, once related this joke in one of his sermons at the Centenary Methodist Church, Hyderabad, India:- A minister once so thoroughly bored the members of his congregation that they finally asked him to quit. "Give me one more chance," he pleaded.

The congregation turned out in force the next Sunday and heard him deliver, to their surprise and delight, the most inspired sermon heard for years.

After the service, everyone shook his hand warmly. One man, an elder of the church, said, "You must stay, with an increase in salary of course."

The minister, accepted. Then the elder said, "That was the greatest sermon I have ever heard. But tell me one thing. As you began to speak you raised two fingers of your left hand, at the end two fingers of your right hand. What was the significance of those gestures?"

"THOSE," answered the minister, "WERE THE QUOTATION MARKS."

29
SIN AND GIN

1. The minister in passing along the street came upon a drunk leaning against a light pole. Thinking he should do his clerical duty he accosted the man thus:

"My friend, I am sorry to see you in this condition. You are in danger of being taken to jail and it is also wrong to do as you are doing."

The drunk looked at the minister inquiringly and said:

"What might your name be, mister?"

"I am the Rev. Paul of the Brethren Church," replied the minister.

The drunk, wholly unconcerned about the prospects of jail or anything else, looked leeringly at the minister and said:

"Shay, Paul, did you ever git any answer to that letter you wrote to them Ephesians?"

☆

2. The Rev Duckley was a young and nervous clergyman and when the time came for him to preach his first sermon, he was somewhat rattled. He stood in the vestry anxiously fingering his collar and wondering if his hair was tidy. Unfortunately there was no mirror in the place. Plucking up courage he asked the verger: "I say, do you think you could get me a glass?"

The verger went out and Duckley waited patiently for his return. He came back hiding something in his coat. Then he drew it out and passed it to the preacher saying cheerfully, "I managed to get a whole bottle by mentioning your name."

☆

3. An old bishop in the nation's capital was sick of the socials and embassy parties he was expected to attend every other afternoon. At one of them he entered wearily, glanced sourly at the over-familiar cast of characters and sank into the nearest chair. The hostess coyly, said, "A spot of tea, Bishop?"

"No tea," growled the Bishop.

"Coffee, Bishop?"

"No coffee."

An understanding woman, she whispered in his ear, "Scotch and water, Bishop?" Said the Bishop brightening, "No water."

☆

4. Father Coogan had finished the Sunday morning service and was shouting at his parishioners. In the middle of the sermon he called out, "Stand up, all ye who prefer sin!"

Quillan, who had been half asleep, jumped to his feet.

"Do you prefer sin?" roared the Priest.

"Oh, I'm sorry! I thought you said 'gin'."

☆

5. There was a parson, full of good works who used to do much jail visit. One day he called in the cell of an 'old lag' and said could he do anything for the man.

The man said yes, he would like to be read from the Bible, of course.

"What would you like me to read?"

"The 119th Psalm, please parson."

"My goodness, brother, that's the longest psalm in the whole Bible."

"Nemmind, parson, I likes it."

So the good man read it over to him, and when he had finished, the old rascal said please could he have the psalm read it to him all over again.

The parson said, "Yes, of course, I take it you have found true religion at last brother?"

"Well, it's not exactly that, but you see, I haven't had a drink for three years and the smell of your breath's doing me a power O' good."

☆

6. A tavern keeper owned a parrot whose perch was upon the piano. One night the tavern burned down and the parrot flew into a nearby church, and perched on the organ. Next

morning when the organist arrived, the parrot replied, "Ha, new pianist." When the congregation came in, the parrot replied, "But all of the same old faces."

☆

7. The priest met Mary O'brien and asked what she was concealing under her cape. She said it was holy water. The priest reached for the bottle, uncorked it and sniffed. "Why, Mary," he exclaimed, "this isn't holy water; this is gin."

Whereupon Mary crossed herself and said, "Glory be to God, another miracle."

☆

8. Simon came along, and as was his habit after a hard day's work, he was going to have a quick one before dinner. A young minister who happened to be there, took him by the arm and said, "Don't go in that place, my brother. The potions you seek will curdle your stomach."

Simon said "You don't say" and continued on.

The young minister followed him and said, "Have you ever seen what that stuff does to worms?"

Simon said, "I'm no worm — I'm master in my own house."

Just as he reached the door, the minister said, "Don't you know, when you go in there, the devil goes with you?"

"Well, if he does, he pays for his own drink!"

☆

9. There was a colonel in Dublin Ohio who sure liked to have his liquor. Nobody thought anything about it, though — he goes to church and even leads the choir. Once a temperance speaker was talking at the church where the colonel had his membership. The speaker said at the start of his speech, "If I had my way, I'd take all the liquor in Dublin county and pour it in the river."

Later on, he waved his hands around and announced, "If I had my way, I'd take all liquor in Ohio and pour it in the river."

Finally for his finish, he thundered, "if I had my way I'd take all the liquor in the world and pour it in the river."

Just then the colonel got up and said to the choir, "We shall now sing, 'Shall we gather at the River'?"

☆

10. A confirmed drunkard had at long last been cured of the bottle and his minister was about to test him to see if the cure was complete. "Now then," he said, "what does the name Gordon convey to you?"

The ex-drunk thought. "Wasn't that the name of a famous general?" he said.

"Very good," said the minister. 'And what does the name Haig mean?"

"He was a noted earl," was the reply.

"Excellent," said the minister. "And now for the supreme test. What does Vat 69 mean to you?"

The man sat in deep thought. At last he looked up. "Isn't that the Pope's telephone number?" he asked.

☆

11. A minister was known by a few of his parishioners to be fond of cherry brandy and one of them in a mischievous frame of mind offered to present him with a bottle on condition that it was fully acknowledged in the next issue of the church magazine. The offer was promptly accepted and in due course the notice appeared in the Magazine:- "The Vicar thanks Mr Mctavish for his gift of fruit and the spirit in which it is given."

☆

12. WINE AND WATER

Old Noah he had an ostrich farm and fowls on the largest scale,

He ate his egg with a ladle in an egg-cup big as a pail.

And the soup he took was Elephant Soup and the fish he took was Whale,

But they all were small to the cellar he took when he set out to sail,

And Noah he often said to his wife when he sat down to dine,

"I don't care where the water goes if it doesn't get into the wine."

155

13. According to local grapevine, Dr Norman Vincent Peale was wounded mentally at least on one occasion. A drunken young man addressed the author of THE POWER OF POSITIVE THINKING: "I want to know," he lisped, "What is the difference between positive and negative thinking?"

Dr Peale was very polite. "Young man" he is supposed to have answered, "if you will ask me that when you are sober, I shall be happy to tell you."

"That's the trouble," the young man mouthed. "When I'm sober, I just don't give a damn."

☆

14. A minister answered his telephone to hear a woman's voice request, "Send six cases of vodka to my house, please."

The pastor recognised the voice as that of one of his parishioners. Gently replied, "I am your minister."

He expected an apology by her for dialling the wrong number. Instead she retorted almost angrily, "What are you doing at the liquor store?"

☆

15. Two deacons were having a social drink at a bar when they saw their preacher go by. One of them became very upset. "I surely hope he didn't see us," he said.

"What difference does it make?" his friend replied. "God knows we're in here."

"I know," said the first deacon, "but God won't tell my wife."

☆

16. Reverend Walford was assailed by a teetotalling preacher for his liberal views about drinking. The minister countered by replying, "There are two drinks mentioned in the Bible, wine: WHICH GLADDENETH THE HEART OF MAN, and water: WHICH QUENCHETH THE THIRST OF JACK-ASSES."

☆

17. There was an Irishman hastening up and down a train, putting his head in every compartment and asking for

a priest. He was clearly distressed and when he came back a second time, a Methodist minister, looked up from the Church Herald and said, "We are all brothers in the Lord, although I am only a humble Methodist preacher. If you will take me to your friend, who is ill or distressed, I will comfort him as well as I may."

"It's meeself that's after bein distressed," said the Irishman, "and no one else besides."

"What can I do, brother?"

"Nothing! I must have a priest. I'm stuck for a bottle opener."

☆

18. It came to the vicar's ears that his organist was in the habit of visiting a pub for a quick one, after playing the organ at eventime. He made a point of speaking to the young man about it. His stern approach met with a most unexpectedly apt quotation from one of the vicar's sermons. "It's like this," said the organist, "I thirst after righteousness."

157

11

30
SPOONERISMS

1. A lady parishioner during a church service sat in the pew which was meant for Rev William Archibald Spooner of Oxford University. Spooner politely said, "Pardon me, madam, but you are occupewing my pie. May I sew you to another sheet?" When a lady told Rev Spooner that his was a beautiful church, the great divine replied, "Many thinkle peep so." One of the amusing spoonerisms describes the good divine's anger with a lazy student. "You are a disgrace," said Spooner, "you have hissed all my mystery lectures. You have in fact tasted a whole worm."

There is another interesting tale of how Dr Spooner became engaged to the daughter of the Bishop of Carisle. The young girl fell in love with the great divine and became engaged to him as a result of his innocent remark at a tea party, "and now my dear lady, will you take me", when he had merely meant, "Make tea."

The great Oxford don who did talk of the Lord as being a 'shoving leopard', once greeted his venerable maiden aunt with, "I am delighted to see you, looking as hairless and cappy as ever."

☆

2. Once Spooner prayed "O Lord, in whose hand is the 'King of Hearts' instead of the heart of kings. Once he said, "It's easier for a camel to go through the knee of the Idol" instead of through the eye of the needle. To a former undergraduate, he said, "I remember your name perfectly, but I just cannot think of your face." In a college sermon: "Which of us has not felt in his heart a half warmed fish?" Proposing a toast: "Let us drink to the queer old dean."

☆

3. When the bishop visited the remote village, the odd lad about the house was told that in the morning he must take up hot water for shaving, knock on the door, and say, "It's the boy, My Lord."

The next morning nerves were unsettled. In answer to his timid knock, the visitor said, "Who is there?"

"It's the Lord, with your water, my boy."

☆

4. Many people, especially the nuns, get nervous when they have to address a bishop as 'My Lord'. Once a nun was giving a bishop a cup of coffee and the bishop could see she was worried. She pushed the coffee cup at the bishop, then the sugar bowl. "How many lords, my lump?" she said.

☆

5. The associate pastor of a church in a large city, at a denominational dinner got a little nervous and confused, even though following the written order of program which listed prayer by Rev John Crow. Turning to his senior pastor he said, "I request Rev Pray to please crow for us."

☆

6. The bridegroom, who was in a horribly nervous condition, appealed to the clergyman in a loud whisper, at the close of the ceremony, "Is it kisstomary to cuss the bride?"

The clergyman replied, "Not yet, soon."

☆

7. The famous Dr Spooner called on the Dean of Christ Church and inquired, "Is the bean dizzy?"

31

SUNDAY SCHOOLS

1. It was Sunday morning in the men's class in a church. "Will you please tell me," said a member to the teacher. "How far in actual miles Dan is from Beersheba? All my life I have heard the familiar phrase 'from Dan to Beersheba', but I have never known the distance."

Another member, "Do I understand that Dan and Beersheba are names of places?"

"Yes," said the teacher.

"That is one on me," continued the man. "I always thought they were husband and wife like Sodom and Gomorrah."

☆

2.   A gorgeous voluptuous creature,
        Seduced a young Methodist preacher,
            It worked out well,
            For under his spell,
        This gal's now a Sunday School teacher.

☆

3.   Our Vicar's an absolute lamb,
        But when he sat in the Jam,
            On taking his seat,
            At our Sunday School treat,
        We all heard the poor man say,
        "Stand up while I say grace."

☆

4. "King Solomon," declared a little girl in Sunday School, "is my favourite character in the Bible — because he was so kind to ladies and animals." The startled teacher demanded, "Who told you that?" "Nobody told me; I read it myself in the Bible" asserted the girl. "It says Solomon kept seven hundred wives and three hundred porcupines."

☆

5.   A new Sunday School teacher had to iron out some prob-

lems with the Lord's Prayer. One child had to be corrected after repeating, "Howard be thy name." Another youngster prayed, "Lead us not into Penn Station." Still another surprised the teacher with, "Our Father, who art in Heaven, How'd you know my name?"

☆

6. The new pastor of a rural church dropped into a Sunday School class and began quizzing the students to test the effectiveness of the teacher.

"Who knocked down the walls of Jericho?" he demanded of one boy.

"It sure wasn't me, Reverend," the boy said.

Turning to the embarrassed teacher, the pastor exclaimed, "I suppose, that's a sample of the kind of discipline you maintain!"

"Now, Reverend, Timmy's a good boy and doesn't tell lies. If he said that he didn't do it, I believe him."

Thoroughly upset, the pastor took the matter to the church's board of deacons. After due consideration, the board sent the following message to the non-plussed minister: "We see no point in making an issue of this incident. The board will pay for the damages to the wall and charge it off to vandalism."

☆

7. A Sunday School teacher after telling the story of the birth of Jesus, decided to test the attentiveness of her pupils. Expecting a reply of either 'The Shepherd' or 'The Wise Men', she asked, "Who was the first to know of Jesus' birth?"

At once a four-year old girl stood up and cried out: "Mary!"

☆

8. Some years ago, George Bernard Shaw was persuaded by a minister friend to visit his Sunday School class. The children in the group had been learning at the time about Daniel in the lion's den.

"Why wasn't Daniel eaten by the lions?" Shaw enquired.

The rector was confident of his charges even before so distinguished a visitor as Shaw, for he had instructed them carefully.

"Because he was a good man," replied one youngster.

"Because Daniel prayed to God," offered another.

To a whole series of replies along these lines Shaw shook his head, and then said, "I am sorry, you are all wrong, children. Daniel was not eaten by the lion because he was a vegetarian — and if you become vegetarians the lions will not eat you either."

☆

9. A DARKY SUNDAY SCHOOL

Jonah was an immigrant, so runs the Bible tale, He took
    a steerage passage in a transatlantic whale
Now, Jonah, in the belly of the whale was quite com-
    pressed.
So Jonah pressed the button, and the whale he did the
    rest.

CHORUS

Young folks, old folks, everybody come,
Join our darky Sunday School, and make yourself to him,
There's a place to check your chewing gum and razors at
    the door,
And hear such Bible stories as you never heard before.

Adam was the first man that ever was invented,
He lived all his life and he never was contented,
He was made out of mud in the days gone by
And hung on the fence in the sun to get him dry.

The good book says Cain killed his brother Abel,
He hit him on the head with a leg of a table,
Then along came Jonah in the belly of the whale,
The first submarine boat that ever did sail.

Esau was a cowboy of the wild and woolly make,
Half the farm belonged to him and half to Brother Jake,
Now, Esau thought his title to the farm was one too clear,
So he sold it to brother for a sandwich and a beer.

Noah was mariner who sailed around the sea,
With half a dozen wives and a big menagerie;
He failed the first season when it rained forty days,
For in that sort of weather no circus ever pays.

Elijah was a prophet who attended country fairs,
He advertised his business with a pair of dancing bears,
He held a sale of prophesies most every afternoon,
And went up in the evening in painted fire balloon.

Then down came Peter, the Keeper of Gates,
He came down cheap on excursion rates,
Then along came Noah a-stumblin' in the dark,
He found a hatchet and some nails and built himself an ark.

David was a shepherd and a scrappy little cuss,
Along came Goliath, just a-spoilin' for a muss,
Now David didn't want to fight, but thought he must or bust,
So he cotched up a cobblestone and busted in his crust.

Ahab had a wife, and her name was Jezebel;
She went out in the vineyard to hang the clothes and fell,
She's gone to the dogs, the people told the king;
Ahab said he'd never heard of such an awful thing.

Samson was a strong man of John L. Sullivan school,
He slew ten thousand Philistines with the jawbone of a mule,
But Delilah captured him and filled him full, of gin,
Slashed off his hair and the coppers run him in.

Samson was a Husky guy as everyone should know,
He used to lift five hundred pounds as strongman in his show,
One week the bill was rotten, all the actors had a souse,
But the strong-man act of Samson's it just brought down
the house.

Salome was a chorus girl who had a winning way,
She was the star attraction in King Herod's cabaret,
Although you can hardly say discretion was her rule,
She's the favourite Bible figure in the
Gertrude Hoffman School.

There are plenty of these Bible tales, I'll tell tomorrow.
How Lot, his wife and family fled from Sodom and Gomorrah,
But his wife she turned to rubber and got stuck upon the spot,
And became a salty monument and missed a happy Lot.

Now Joey was unhappy in the Bowels of the soil,
He lost his pretty rainbow coat because he wouldn't toil.
He hollered, howled, and bellowed until far into the night,
But of course, you couldn't see him, for he was out of sight.

It happened that a caravan was passing by the place,
Laden down with frankincence and imitation lace,
They heard the sheeny yelling and pulled him from the well,
If that ain't a proper ending, then you can go to hell.

☆

10. The Sunday School teacher was showing off her pupils
for the benefit of a visitor, and trying to grade her questions
to their intelligence so that each one would make a good
showing.

"Johnny," she said to a dumb little brat, "Is there anything that God can't do?"

"Yes, Ma'am," said Johnny confidently.

"Now think again," said the teacher. "I asked if there was
anything that God could not do."

"Yes, Ma'am, there is," came the reply as emphatic as
before.

"Well, what is it?" asked the teacher in exasperation.

Replied Johnny triumphantly, "He cannot please everybody."

11. The young Sunday School teacher clearly explained to the children the meaning of this text from Genesis 28:12: "And he lighted upon a certain place, and tarried there all night, because the sun was set; and he took of the stones of that place, and put them for his pillows, and lay down in that place to sleep. And he dreamed, and behold a ladder set up on the earth, and the top of it reached to heaven: and behold the angels of God ascending and descending on it." After explaining the text, she asked if there were any questions.

"If the lovely angels had wings," asked a ten-year-old boy, "Why did they have to climb up and down the old ladder for?"

The teacher cleared her throat and said, "Are there any more questions?"

☆

12. The teacher of a Sunday School class explained the story of how Prophet Elijah built the altar, put wood upon it, and cut the bullock into pieces and laid them on the altar.

"And then," the teacher said, "he commanded the people to fill four barrels with water and pour it over the altar, and they did this four times. Now children, can any one of you tell why this water was poured over the bullock on the altar?"

A shrill voice from the back rows said, "To make the gravy!"

☆

13. Little Mary in Sunday School listened intently while the teacher told about Heaven. She concluded by saying, "All who are glad you are going to Heaven, raise your hands." Every hand went up except one. "Why don't you want to go to Heaven, Mary?" asked the teacher. "Well," Mary replied, "When I left home, Mom was baking an apple pie."

32

TEN COMMANDMENTS

1. What a scarcity of news would there be if everybody obeyed the Ten Commandments.

☆

2. The Ten Commandments were given to men in tablet form, and by following their direction, we could save a lot of other tablets from being used.

☆

3. When the Lord gave us Ten Commandments, He didn't mention amendments.

☆

4. The United States Supreme Court has handed down the Eleventh Commandment: "Thou shalt not, in thy classroom, read the first ten."

☆

5. Man is an able creature, but he has made 32,600,000 laws and hasn't yet improved on the Ten Commandments.

☆

6. Some one has tabulated that we have put 35 million laws in the books trying to enforce the Ten Commandments.

☆

7. "I have good news and I have bad news," spoke Moses as he returned from the peaks of Mount Sinai. "The good news is that God has reduced the Commandments to ten. The bad news is that adultery is still in."

☆

8. A bishop asked a small boy what he knew about the Ten Commandments. "Not much," was the reply. "I've only seen the trailer."

9. A man entered the post office with a package containing a Bible. The postal attendant looked over the tightly wrapped parcel, and asked, "Is there anything breakable in this?"

"Nothing but the Ten Commandments" was the reply.

☆

10. An old chieftain was being evangelised by a missionary. Noting that the men had the habit of filing their teeth to sharp points, the missionary put emphasis on the 'THOU SHALT NOT.' Patiently the aged chieftain listened.

"You mean that I must not take my neighbour's wife."

"That's correct," said the missionary.

"Or his oxen, or his elephants."

"That's right."

"Or I must not dance the war dance and then ambush him on the road and kill him.

"So right."

"Then I can become a good Christian," sighed the chieftain, "for I cannot do any of these things. I am old."

☆

11. An enthusiastic church member said to her pastor, "I'm so anxious to make a trip to the Holy Land, climb to the top of Mount Sinai, and shout the Ten Commandments."

The pastor replied, "I've got a better suggestion: stay at home and keep them."

☆

12. LATEST DECALOGUE

Thou shalt have one God only, who
would bear the expense of two?
No graven images may be
worshipped, except the currency.

Swear not at all, for thy curse
Thine enemy is none the worse;
At Church on Sunday to attend
Will serve to keep the world thy friend.

167

Honour thy parents, that is all
From whom advancement may befall
Thou shalt not kill; but needst not strive
Officiously to keep alive.

Do not adultery commit,
Advantage rarely comes of it;
Thou shalt not steal, an empty feat
When it's so lucrative to cheat.

Bear not false witness, let the lie
Have time on its own wings to fly,
Thou shalt not covet, but tradition
Approves all forms of competition.

The sum of all is, thou shalt never labour
More than thyself to love thy neighbour.
— *Arthur Hugh Clough*

13. A man who had lost his hat decided the simplest way to replace it was to go to church and steal one from the cloakroom. Once inside, he heard a sermon on the Ten Commandments. Coming out he was greeted by the minister and said to him, "I want you to know, Reverend, that you saved me from crime. I came here with sin in my heart. I was going to steal a hat, but after hearing your sermon, I changed my mind."

"Fine," exulted the minister. "Would you tell me what I said that led you to change your mind?"

"Well, Reverend, when you got to that part about "Thou shalt not commit adultery', I suddenly remembered where I left my hat."

33

VERSE AND WORSE

1. Isaac Watts, who wrote the immortal hymn, "WHEN I SURVEY THE WONDROUS CROSS ON WHICH THE PRINCE OF GLORY DIED, was a born poet. His father, who was a no nonsense man, was not enamoured of his son's poetic exertions, and severely warned him to stop this balderdash. But poetry was in his veins. One morning, when his family knelt for prayers, Isaac pointed to a mouse running up the bell rope and exclaimed:-

THERE WAS A MOUSE FOR WANT OF STAIRS,
RAN UP A ROPE TO SAY HIS PRAYERS.

The children smiled in amusement. Isaac saw the angry expression on his father's face. He ran to him pleading:
O FATHER, FATHER, PITY TAKE,
AND I WILL NO MORE VERSES MAKE.

2. To the church I once went,
   But I grieved and sorrowed,
   For the season was Lent,
   And the sermon was borrowed.

3. "Attend your church" the pastor cries,
   to church each fair one goes,
   The old go there to close their eyes,
   The young go there to eye their clothes.

☆

4. **A QUARRELSOME BISHOP**
   To hide his ordure, claws the cat,
   You claw but to cover that,
   Be decenter and learn at least,
   one lesson from the cleaner beast
                              — *Lord Francis Jeffrey*

169

5. **ON DR KEENE, BISHOP OF CHESTER**
The Bishop of Chester,
Though wiser than Nestor,
And fairer than Esther
If you scratch him, he will fester.

— Thomas Gay

☆

6. **BISHOP BLOOMFIELD'S FIRST CHARGE
TO HIS CLERGY**
Hunt not, fish not, shoot not,
Dance not, fiddle not, flute not,
Be sure ye have nothing to do with the Whigs,
But stay at home and feed your pigs;
And above all, I make it my special desire,
That at least once a week you dine with the squire.

— *Sydney Smith*

☆

7. **A CLERGYMAN'S HORSE BITING HIM**
The steed bit his master,
How come this to pass?
We heard the good pastor
Cry, "All hell is grass."

☆

8. **THE PARSON'S LOOKS**
That there is falsehood in his looks,
I must and will deny;
They say their master is a knave—
And sure they do not lie.

☆

9. **KING DAVID & KING SOLOMON**
King David and King Solomon
Led merry merry lives,
With many many lady friends,
And many many wives.
But when old age crept over them

170

With many many qualms,
King Solomon wrote the Proverbs,
King David wrote the Psalms.

— James Ball Naylor

10. UPON SAUL SEEKING HIS ASSES

Saul did much care and diligence express
By seeking asses in the wilderness,
Three days he travelled with a serious mind,
to find them out, could no asses find,
Find out a hundred you in London may,
Of Presbyterian asses in one day.

11. ON THE DEATH OF A FEMALE OFFICER
OF THE SALVATION ARMY

Hallelujah was the only observation,
That escaped Lieutenant-Colonel Mary Jane,
When she tumbled off the platform on the station,
And was cut in little pieces by the train.
Mary Jane, the train is through her, Hallelujah!
Hallelujah!
We will gather up the fragments that remain.

12. WHAT A PREACHER OUGHT TO KNOW

One thing a preacher
Should remember for sure
The mind can absorb
Only what the seat can endure.

13. ON A THEOLOGIAN

A young theologian named Twiddle,
refused to accept his degree,
He said, "It's enough being Twiddle,
without being Twiddle D.D."

171

14. METHUSELAH

Methuselah ate what he found on his table,
And never as people do now
Did he note the amount of the calorie count;
He ate it because it was chow.

He was not disturbed as at dinner he sat,
Devouring a roast or a pie,
To think it was lacking in granular fat,
Or a couple of vitamins shy.

He cheerfully chewed each species of food,
unmindful of troubles or fears,
lest his health might be hurt,
by some fancy dessert;
and he lived over 900 years.

— *Author unknown*

15. Enthusiasts, Lutherans, and monks,
Jews, Syndics, Calvinists, and punks,
Gibbon an atheist call,
While he, unhurt, in placid mood,
To prove himself a Christian good,
Kindly forgives them all.

16. He'll find the empty pews are few
When Sunday sermon time is due—
The man who can exhort his flock
In twenty minutes by the clock.

17. THE MINISTER IN THE PULPIT

The minister in the pulpit
He couldn't say his prayers,
He laughed and he giggled,
And he fell down the stairs,
The stairs gave a crack,
And he broke his humpy back,
And all the congregation,
Went 'quack, quack, quack.'

172

18. A man may cry church! at every word,
    With no more piety than other people;
    A daw's not reckoned a religious bird
    Because it keeps acawing from the steeple.

One day he (Jonathan Swift) was sheltering himself under a tree during a storm and along came a young couple who took cover beside him. Seeing that the stranger wore a clergyman's attire, they told him that they were on their way to get married.

"I'll marry you here and now," said the great Dean of St Patrick's Cathedral. And what's more he did it in verse, extemporaneous and witty:

> In stormy weather
> I join these two together,
> Let none but He who rolls the thunder,
> Part this man and woman asunder.

☆

19. **THE MAN WITH THE CONSECRATED CAR**
    He couldn't speak before a crowd;
    He couldn't teach a class;
    But when he came to Sunday School
    He brought the folks 'en masse'.

    He couldn't sing to save his life;
    In public couldn't pray;
    But always his 'jalopy' was
    Just crammed on each Lord's Day.

    And though he couldn't sing, nor teach,
    Nor even lead in prayer,
    He listened well; he had a smile,
    And he was always there—

    With all the others whom he brought
    Who lived near and far—
    And God's work was greatly prospered
    For he had a consecrated car.

173

20. BEELZEBUB

Sly Beelzebub took all occasions
To try Job's constancy and patience.
He took his honour, took his health,
His servants, oxen, horse, cows—
But cunning Satan did NOT take his spouse.

But Heaven, that brings out good from evil,
And loves to disappoint the devil,
And prestined to restore
TWOFOLD all he had before;
His servants, horses, oxen, cows—
Short-sighted devil, not to take his spouse.

— *Samuel Taylor Coleridge.*

34

WIT & SARCASM

1. A horse-trader once said to Henry Ward Beecher, "I have a good family horse I want to sell you. He is a good carriage horse. He works double with any other horse and on either side of the tongue. In short, he is a good all round horse and a good team worker."

Dr Beecher replied, "My friend, I can't buy your horse, but I would like to have him as a member of my church."

☆

2. Canon Sydney Smith was a frequent guest at the home of poet Samuel Rogers. Whenever the witty clergyman was invited for dinner, Samuel Rogers used to place candles all round the dining room and high up, in order to show off the pictures. Once he asked Sydney Smith how he liked the arrangement of the candles.

"Not at all," replied Smith, "above, there is a maze of lights, and below nothing but gnashing of teeth."

☆

3. A Scotman was travelling in the Holy Land, and when he came to the Sea of Galilee, he saw a boatman standing beside a board which advertised trips in a pleasure boat. Wishing to see the sights, the Scotman asked the boatman how much he charged. He was told the fee would be the equivalent of five pounds. The Scotman said indignantly, "D'you know that in Glasgow I can hire a boat for a week for that much money?" The boatman shrugged and said, "But these are the waters upon which our Lord walked." The Scotman turned away and said, "Nae wonder He walked."

☆

4. Dean Inge was delighted by an angry letter he had received from a lady who disagreed with one of his articles. "I am praying nightly for your death," she wrote. "It may interest you to know that in two cases I have had great success."

After his retirement from the Deanery, he became a regular contributor to a London Journal and told us, with a chuckle, of the critical comment that he had ceased to be a pillar of the church, and was now two columns of the Evening Standard!"   — *Alfred Noyes*

☆

5. A few days before Easter Sunday, a pastor sent a newsletter to his parishioners requesting all to attend the Easter Service — whether with the traditional New Easter outfit or not. The next day his phone rang steadily as the congregants pointed out with malicious glee that he had written: FORGET YOUR CLOTHES AND COME TO CHURCH ON EASTER SUNDAY."

☆

6. Rt Rev & Rt Hon Graham Douglas Leonard, Bishop of London, was gracious enough to send me this interesting story. It is about a bishop who was retiring. In the city of his diocese a daily evening paper was published. The bishop was asked to a great many dinners so that people could say farewell to him. On one occasion he was about to tell a story but before doing so, he turned to the press who were present and said, "As I think you know, I am dining tomorrow with such and such an organisation, I would like to use this story again so I would appreciate it if you didn't make any reference in your paper tomorrow." When the paper was published next day the report of the dinner included these words: "at this point in his speech the bishop told a story which we are sorry we are unable to print."

☆

7. A miserly tycoon asked a famed 18th century artist to do a giant-sized painting of the destruction of the Egyptians in the Red Sea. The artist agreed, but the fee offered him was so scanty that he demanded payment in advance. When the painting was finally delivered, the miser was filled with fury at beholding a blank, large square of canvas. He rushed to the artist's studio in a rage.

"You," he cried, "have cheated me! Where are the Israelites?"

"Why," was the answer, "they have already crossed over."

"And I see no Egyptians," fumed the skinflint.

"As you well know," retorted the cunning artist, "they have all drowned."

☆

8. Mother of Lester Pearson, former Prime Minister of Canada, was a devout Christian whose greatest desire was that her son should study theology and become a minister in the church. But as luck would have it, Pearson joined politics and in course of time was elected Prime Minister of Canada. Immediately after his election, he sent a telegram to his mother, "Mom, at last I have become a minister!"

Mrs Pearson wired back, "Second class minister, not first class minister."

☆

9. I am grateful to Kariel Gardosh (Dosh), one of the greatest satirists of Israel for sending me this piece on pious liars. This is about a not so devoted Jew who on the Holy Day of Atonement decides to pay a call on the synagogue. But the place is crowded and he has not made the necessary reservation. So he addressed the usher at the gate: "Please let me in — it's just for a few minutes. I have to say something important to my brother-in-law."

The usher answers: You rascal! You want to pray!

☆

10. A man named Prophet Jones calls his form of faith, which has grown into a large organisation, 'The House of God'. This colourful Negro minister has done so well selling God that he is able to live in fabulous luxury.

When the prophet went to London recently he took an entire floor at the expensive Dorchester House Hotel in Park Lane, arriving with a large suite of assistants. After the first week of his stay he paid his bill with a cheque signed by himself over the imprint of 'The House of God' but due to a technical error the cheque was returned by the bank to the hotel management. A witty bank-clerk had written on it: "Refer to Maker."

177

11. Around two O'clock on a cold, stormy night, the phone rang at the rectory. Father Kelly lifted the phone to hear a voice say "I think Grandma is dying." As it was only a stone's throw from the rectory, Father Kelly decided to go by foot. As he entered a lane, a fellow with a gun stepped out and shouted, "Handover your money purse." The priest said that his pocketbook was in his coat and then opened his coat to take out the purse, revealing his clerical collar. "Oh, I didn't know you were a priest," stammered the gunman. "Excuse me, Father, I don't need your money."

Greatly relieved, Fr Kelly offered a cigar but the fellow refused to take and said "No, thanks, Father. I don't smoke during Lent."

☆

12. A lady in a Pentecostal congregation was in the habit of shouting loud, 'hallelujas and praise-the-Lords' disturbing the solemn church service. On one Sunday morning, as she resorted to too much shouting of 'hallelujas and praise-the-Lords', two hefty ushers carried her out. As she was finally taken down the aisle, she exclaimed, "I can't stand the honour! I can't stand the honour!" When a fellow congregant asked what she meant by that, she cried out, "My Lord was carried into Jerusalem on the back of one jackass. I have the honour of being carried by two!"

☆

13. The noted American Clergyman and orator, Henry Ward Beecher had a speaking engagement in a small town. A few minutes before he was to speak, he went into a barber shop for a shave. The barber not knowing who he was, asked if he was going to hear Beecher speak.

"I guess so," said Beecher.

"I am afraid," said the barber, "The tickets are sold out and you may have to stand."

"That's just my luck," said Beecher, "I always have to stand when I hear that gentleman talk!"

178

14.   A STATEMENT OF COSTS

The painter was required to render an itemised bill for
his repairs on various pictures in the church. The statement
was as follows:-

Corrected and renewed the Ten Commandments.	$ 50
Embellished Pontius Pilate and put a new ribbon on his bonnet.	$ 60
Put a new tail on the rooster of St Peter and mended his bill	$ 45
Put a new nose on St John the Baptist and straightened his eye.	$ 25
Replumed and gilded the left wing of the Guardian Angel.	$ 65
Washed the servant of the High Priest and put carims on his cheeks.	$ 25
Renewed Heaven, adjusted ten stars, gilded the sun, cleansed the moon.	$ 85
Reanimated the flames of Purgatory and restored some souls.	$ 45
Revived the flames of Hell, put a new tail on the Devil, mended his left hoof, and did several odd jobs for the damned.	$ 65
Put new spatter-dashes on the son of Tobias and dressing on his sack.	$ 30
Rebordered the robe of Herod and readjusted his wig.	$ 45
Cleansed the ears of Balaam's ass and shod him.	$ 35
Put earrings in the ears of Sarah.	$ 70
Put a new stone in David's sling, enlarged Goliath's hand, and extended his legs.	$ 30
Decorated Noah's Ark.	$ 20
Mended the shirt of the Prodigal son, and cleaned the pigs.	$ 15
	$ 710

15. A FUGITIVE FOUND

Feeling footloose and frisky, a featherbrained fellow forced his fond father to fork over the farthings and flew far to foreign fields and frittered his fortune feasting fabulously with faithless friends.

Fleeced by his fellows in folly and facing famine he found himself a feed flinger in a filthy farm. Fairly famishing, he fain would have filled his frame with foraged food from fodder fragments. "Fooey, my father's flunkies fare far finer!"

The frazzled fugitive forlornly fumbled, frankly facing facts. He fled forthwith to his family. Falling at his father's feet, he forlornly fumbled. "Father, I've flunked and fruitlessly forfeited family favour".

The farsighted father, forstalling further flinching, frantically flagged the flunkies to fetch a fatling from the flock and fix a feast.

The fugitive's fault-finding brother frowned on fickle forgiveness of the former folderol.

But the faithful father figured, "Filial fidelity is fine, but the fugitive is found! What forbid fervent festivity? Let flags be unfurled! Let fanfares flair!"

☆

16. A minister was stopped on the Interstate for speeding. As most people do, he wanted to argue with the patrolman about how fast he was going. "I sure wasn't going 70 miles an hour," he said. "How did you time my speed? I don't see a radar any place."

"We didn't catch you with radar," the patrolman said. "You were spotted by our helicopter patrol."

"Oh," said the minister. "That's all right then, because I never question anything that comes from above."

☆

17. A Western bookseller wrote to a Chicago firm for a dozen copies of Dean Farrar's 'SEEKERS AFTER GOD' to be sent to him at once. He got a telegram in reply, which read, "NO SEEKERS AFTER GOD" in Chicago or New York. Suggest you try Philadelphia."

18. When the Very Rev Dr William Ralph Inge, the famous Dean of St Paul's was Asst. Master at Eaton, Queen Victoria visited the school. A boy from the school was chosen to welcome the Queen at the solemn function. Ralph Inge sent for the boy and told him, "It is a great honour to have been chosen to make the welcome speech. While it is entirely for you to compose your speech, I decided to leave some thoughts with you. Avoid the temptation of using the superlatives, like, "When the Queen comes, it is sunrise', and "When the Queen goes, it is sunset." Be deferential. Above all, be brief and matter of fact." The young brat got up smartly and made his welcome speech. He said, "We are grateful to Her Majesty, the Queen for finding time to visit our school. Of the queen, the less said the better it is."

35

WITH DUE APOLOGIES
TO THE CLERGY

1. A man of the cloth noticed a bunch of mischievous youngsters clustered around a mongrel. "What are you doing, my beloved children?" he asked, with fatherly concern.

"Exchanging lies," said one of the boys. "The chap that tells the biggest one gets the dog."

"My God!" exclaimed the minister. "Why, when I was of your age I never thought of uttering a lie."

"You win," shouted the urchins in one voice. "The dog is yours, mister."

☆

2. The noted American preacher and lecturer, Henry Ward Beecher once said to Park Benjamin, the famous poet and humorist, "Benjamin, why you never come to hear me preach?"

"Why Beecher, to be violently earnest, I have conscientious scruples against going to places of amusement on Sundays," replied Benjamin.

☆

3. The late Rev Merton Rice, pastor of the Metropolitan Church of Detroit, one morning returned from a trip with only a few coins in his pocket which he gave to the Pullman porter. Unmindful of this, when he was accosted by a beggar, the great preacher invited him with characteristic compassion to be his guest for a breakfast in the station lunch-room.

After a sumptuous meal, Rev Rice got up to pay the bill and was shocked to realise he had nothing in his pocket. The tramp seeing the embarrassing situation, paid for both of them. Highly disconcerted, Dr Rice said, "Come with me in a cab to my house and I will return your money."

"No, you don't," replied the tramp. "You tricked me for a meal, but you can't trick me for the cab fare too."

4. The preacher was getting weary of being disturbed. "I think there are a great many fools here this morning," he said. "Wouldn't it be advisable to hear one at a time?"

"Yes," said a backbencher, "go ahead with your sermon, parson."

☆

5. A conceited clergyman asked an old man how he had enjoyed his sermon. Said the old man, "I liked most the one passage at the end."

"Which one was that?"

"The one from the pulpit to the vestry."

☆

6. Cries Sylvia to a reverend dean,
     "What reason can be given,
 Since marriage is a holy thing.
     Why there is none in Heaven?"

"There are no women," he replied.
     She quick returns the jest—
 "Women there are, but I'm afraid
     They cannot find a priest."

☆

7. Once the famous French philosopher and writer, Francois Voltaire attended a dinner at which a bishop was present. Voltaire was in a very jovial mood and his wit held the audience spellbound. Finally the prelate interrupted, "When will that clown leave preaching?"

The waspish Voltaire shot back, "The moment, my Lord, I am made a bishop."

☆

8. At the meeting of the British Association in 1860, the Bishop of Oxford looking at Thomas Huxley, the expounder of the theory of evolution, said with a derisive smile, "I beg to know, is it through your grandfather or your grandmother that you claim your descent from a monkey."

The audience was horrified. Thomas Huxley's eyes sparkled as he rose to his feet and then dispassionately said,

"If there were an ancestor, I might possibly be ashamed in recalling it would be a man like the Bishop of Oxford."

☆

9. When John William Colenso of Natal, shocked the ecclesiastical hierarchy with his PENTATEUCH AND THE BOOK OF JOSHUA CRITICALLY EXAMINED, he had his Punch Weekly champions. An attempt to have him deposed and excommunicated prompted Shirley Brooke to hurl some pungent banter at jockeying church dignitaries:

THE NATAL CORRESPONDENCE

I

My Dear Colenso,
    With regret,
    We hierarchy, in conclave met,
    Beg you, you most disturbing writer,
    To take off your colonial mitre.

Your most truly,

Lambeth.   LONGLEY.

II

My Dear Archbishop,
    To resign
    That Zulu diocese of mine,
    And own myself a heathen dark,
    Because I've doubts about Noah's Ark,
    Is not the course for.

Yours,

Kensington.   Colenso.

☆

10. I am bathed in gratitude to Bishop James K. Mathews, Washington for sending me this joke: "A bishop arrived at a church. The bell was rung 3 times. The bishop asked why? The answer, 'For an ordinary pastor, we ring the bell, one time; for archdeacon or District Superintendent, two times; for a bishop or other kind of calamity, three times.

184

11. A chaplain who had preached the Azzize sermon failed to obtain, by indirect methods, any compliments from the Judge. At last he asked His Lordship point-blank what he thought of the discourse.

"It was a divine sermon," said Hawkins. "For it was like the peace of God — which passeth all understanding. And like his mercy it seemed to endure for ever."

☆

12. A man had stolen a turkey, and because of his conscience, he visited his minister. "My family was hungry," the man said. "So I stole this turkey. But I feel that I have sinned. Would you please take it?"

"Certainly not," the minister said.

"Then what should I do with it?" the man asked.

"Give it back to the man you stole it from," the minister said.

"I offered it to him," the man said. "But he refused it. Now what should I do?"

"In that case," the minister said, "it would be all right for you to keep it and feed your family."

That seemed to settle things as far as the man was concerned. He said, "Thank you for your help, Sir." He picked up the turkey and hurried away.

Later that afternoon when the minister returned home, he discovered that somebody had stolen his Thanksgiving turkey.

☆

13. After his retirement Sir Charles Frederick Gill, King's Counsel, built himself a beautiful house in the country. The Vicar asked him why he never attended church. This annoyed Gill, whose answer was, "For two very good reasons, Sir. The first is that, as Recorder of Chichester, I am prayed for in the Cathedral every Sunday morning; and the second, that I have defended more clergymen at the Old Bailey than any living barrister."

☆

14. Dr Clifford, the famous preacher, once arrived at

185

service he was to conduct at Carr's Birmingham, only a few minutes before it was due to begin. The policeman at the door refused to admit him. He said the place was full. "But I am Dr Clifford," protested the preacher. "Oh, are you?" said the bobby, with heavy sarcasm. "Well, I've let two Dr Cliffords already."

☆

15. A very old man with a weak heart won fifty thousand pounds in a football pool in England. His family fearing that the glad news might prove fatal, called in the vicar to break it to him. "Now, John," began the vicar cautiously, "supposing you were to win one of these big prizes — fifty thousand pounds, say — what would you do with it?"

The old man pondered. "Well, Sir," he said, "to start with I'd give you half of it for the church."

The Vicar fell dead.

☆

16. The drunken bum, who looked like he had been taking a bath in a gin mixmaster, flopped into the subway seat next to a Priest. His hat was over one ear, his tie torn, he was plastered with a lipstick and a half-empty bottle of gin stuck out of his pocket. He opened his newspaper and began reading.

After a few minutes, the drunk turned to the Priest and asked, "Say, Father, what causes arthritis?"

This was the opening the Priest was looking for. "I'll tell you what causes arthritis, mister," he said. "It's caused by loose living, being with cheap women, too much alcohol and a contempt for your fellowmen."

"Well, I'll be damned," the drunk mumbled, and returned to his newspaper.

The Priest thought about what he had said and felt he had been a little too harsh. He nudged the bum and apologised. "I'm sorry — I didn't mean to come on so strong. How long have you had arthritis?"

"I don't have arthritis," the drunk said, "I was just reading here that the Pope has it."

17. Fulton Sheen relates that shortly after his elevation to the rank of bishop, he made the first of his appearances on television and stopped for a cup of coffee at the drug-store in the building where the studio was located, with his cape already in place. The girl at the counter obviously used to serving actors, took the red cape very much in stride and asked blithely, "What's yours, Cock Robin?"

☆

18. George Ade, motoring in Indiana, ran plumb into a convention of ministers one evening. When they discovered Ade's identity, the ministers clustered round him to shake hands. One asked, "How does a humorist of your stamp, Sir, feel in such a reverend company as this?"

"I feel," admitted Mr Ade, "like a lion in a den of Daniels."

☆

19. The folly of snap judgements of others is well illustrated by the story of the late Bishop Potter of New York. He was sailing for Europe on one of the great transatlantic liners. When he went on board, he found another passenger was to share the cabin with him. After going to see his accommodation he came up to the purser's desk and inquired if he could leave his gold watch and other valuables in the ship's safe. He explained that ordinarily he never availed himself of that privilege but he had been to his cabin and met the man who was to occupy the other berth and judging from his appearance, he was afraid that he might not be a very trustworthy person. The purser accepted the responsibility of caring for the valuables and remarked, "It's all right, Bishop, I'll be very glad to take care of them for you. The other man has been up here and left his for the same reason." (Sunday School Times).

☆

20. Bishop Doane of Albany was at one time rector of an Episcopal church in Hartford, and Mark Twain, who occasionally attended his services, played a joke on him one Sunday.

"Dr Doane," he said at the end of the service, "I enjoyed your service this morning. I welcomed it like an old friend. I have, you know, a book at home containing every word of it."

187

"You have not," said Dr Doane.

"I have so."

"Well, send that book to me. I'd like to see it."

"I'll send it," the humorist replied.

Next morning he sent an unabridged dictionary to the rector.

☆

21. Two parsons were having lunch at a farm during the progress of certain anniversary celebrations. The farmer's wife cooked a couple of chickens, saying that the family could dine on the remains after the visitors had gone. But the hungry parsons wolfed the chickens bare.

Later the farmer was conducting the guests round the farm, when an old rooster commenced to crow ad lib. "Seems mighty proud of himself," said one of the guests.

"No wonder," growled the farmer, "he's got two sons in the ministry."

SOURCES AND
ACKNOWLEDGEMENTS

I ABSENT - MINDED CLERGYMEN

10. Leslie & Bernice Flynn, HUMOROUS NOTES, QUOTES AND ANECDOTES (1973). Page 102. Reprinted by permission of Baker Book House, Grand Rapids, Michigan.

11. Lewis & Faye Copeland, 10,000 JOKES, TOASTS & STORIES. Copyright 1939,1940 by Lewis & Faye Copeland and Copyright (C) 1965 by Doubleday, a division of Bantam, Doubleday, Dell Publishing Group, Inc. Reprinted by permission of the publishers. Page 501.

II ADAM AND EVE

12. Peter Cagney, THE BOOK OF WIT AND HUMOUR (1976). Reprinted by permission of Thorsons Publishers Limited, U.K. Page 234.

15. Steven Lukes & Itzhak Galnoor, NO LAUGHING MATTER (1985). Reprinted by permission of Routledge & Kegan Paul, U.K. (1985). Page 108.

20-21. Tal D. Bonham, THE TREASURY OF CLEAN CHURCH JOKES (Nashville Broadman Press, 1986). Pages 15 and 17. All rights reserved. Used by permission.

III ARCHBISHOPS

2. Reprinted by permission of WASHINGTON POST.

3. Patrick Mahony, BARBED WIT & MALICIOUS HUMOR (1956). Reprinted by permission of The Institute for the Study of Man, Washington. Page 178.

7. Israel H. Weisfeld, THE PULPIT TREASURY OF WIT & HUMOR (1950). Published by Prentice-Hall Inc., New York. Pages 34-35.

8. Patrick Mahony, BARBED WIT & MALICIOUS HUMOR (1956). Reprinted by permission of The Institute for The Study of Man, Washington. Pages 154-155.

10. Murray Watts, ROLLING IN THE AISLES (1987). Reprinted by permission of Monarch Publications Limited, East Sussex, U.K. Page 47.

IV BAPTISMS

2. Peter Cagney, THE BOOK OF WIT & HUMOUR (1976). Printed by permission of Thorsons Publishers Ltd. U.K. Page 301.

189

13

4. Larry Wilde, THE LAST OFFICIAL IRISH JOKE BOOK, Bantam Books (1983). Reprinted by permission of Larry Wilde. Page 100.

5. William R. Gerler, THE EXECUTIVE'S TREASURY FOR EVERY OCCASION (1967). Reprinted by permission of William R. Gerler. Pages 198-199.

6. Bennett Cerf, THE LAUGH'S ON ME (1959). Reprinted by permission of Doubleday, a division of Bantam, Doubleday, Dell Publishing Group Inc. Pages 351-352.

7. Anthony P. Castle, QUOTES & ANECDOTES. Reprinted by permission of St. Paul Publications, Bandra, Bombay. Pages 166-167.

8. Bennett Cerf, THE LIFE OF THE PARTY (1956). Reprinted by permission of Doubleday, a division of Bantam, Doubleday, Dell Publishing Group, Inc. Pages 87-88.

9. Lewis & Faye Copeland, 10,000 JOKES, TOASTS & STORIES. Copyright 1939, 1940 by Lewis & Faye Copeland and Copyright (c) 1965 by Doubleday, a division of Bantam, Doubleday, Dell Publishing Group, Inc. Reprinted by permission of the publishers. Page 502.

10-11. Patrick Mahony. BARBED WIT & MALICIOUS HUMOR (1956). Reprinted by permission of the Institute for the Study of Man, Washington. Pages 32 and 134-135.

13. Laugh Magazine No. 230, Page 28.

15. Tal D. Bonham. THE TREASURY OF CLEAN CHURCH JOKES (Nashville-Broadman Press 1986). Page 98. All rights reserved. Used by permission.

V THE BIBLE

17. Herbert V. Prochnow and Herbert V. Prochnow Jr., QUOTATIONS FOR ALL OCCASIONS. (1983). Reprinted by permission of Thorsons Publishers Limited, U.K. Pages 351-352.

18. Steven Lukes & Itzhak Galnoor, NO LAUGHING MATTER (1985). Reprinted by permission of Routledge & Kegan Paul, U.K. Page 112.

19. Herbert V. Prochnow & Herbert V. Prochnow Jr., THE PUBLIC SPEAKER'S TREASURE CHEST (1977). Reprinted by permission of Thorsons Publishers Ltd. U.K. Pages 296-297.

20. Herbert V. Prochnow & Herbert V. Prochnow, THE PUBLIC SPEAKER'S TREASURE CHEST (1977). Reprinted by permission of Routledge & Kegan Paul. Pages 101-102.

21-22. Patrick Mahony, BARBED WIT & MALICIOUS HUMOUR

(1956). Reprinted by permission of the Institute for The Study of Man, Washington. Pages 84 and 92.

VI CARDINAL WIT

1-2. Rev Fr Mauricio Rufino, A VADEMECUM OF STORIES (1972). Printed by permission of St. Paul Publications, Bandra, Bombay. India. Pages 497 & 704.

3. Fred M. Pais, SMILES & CHUCKLES, published by Asian Trading Corporation, Bangalore.

4. Marjorie Barrow, Mathilda Schimer and Bannett Cerf, THE TREASURY OF HUMOUR & TOASTMASTER'S HAND-BOOK. Published by Groiler Inc., New York

6-7. Israel H. Weisfeld, THE PULPIT TREASURY OF WIT & HUMOR (1950). Published by Prentice-Hall, Inc., New York. Pages 27 and 19.

9. Khushwant Singh's JOKE BOOK (1987). Published by Orient Paperbacks, New Delhi, India. Page 65.

10. Patrick Mahony, BARBED WIT & MALICIOUS HUMOR (1956). Printed by permission of The Institute for The Study of Man, Washington. Page 175.

VII CATHOLICS & PROTESTANTS

1. Des MacHale, MORE OF THE WORLD'S BEST IRISH JOKES (1985). Reprinted by permission of Angus and Robertson, U.K.

3. Leslie & Bernice Flynn, HUMOROUS NOTES, QUOTES & ANECDOTES (1973). Reprinted by permission of Baker Book House, Grand Rapids, Michigan. Page 165.

4. Steven Lukes & Itzhak Galnoor, NO LAUGHING MATTER (1985). Reprinted by permission of Routledge & Kegan Paul, U.K. Page 85.

5. Kenneth Edwards, I WISH I'D SAID THAT! (1976). Reprinted by permission of Blackie & Son, U.K. Page 24.

6. Marjorie Barrow, Mathilda Schirmer & Bennett Cerf, THE TREASURY OF HUMOR & TOASTMASTER'S HAND-BOOK ( ). Published by Groiler Inc., New York. Pages 477-478.

8. From the book COMPLETE SPEAKER'S GALAXY OF FUNNY STORIES, JOKES AND ANECDOTES by WINSTON K. PENDLETON (c) 1979. Used by permission of the publisher, Parker Publishing Company, Inc., West Nyack, N.Y. Page 195.

VIII CHRISTIANS & JEWS

1. Des MacHale, MORE OF WORLD'S BEST IRISH JOKES (1985). Reprinted by permission of Angus & Robertson, U.K.
2. RUGBY JOKES SCORE AGAIN (1987). Reprinted by permission of Sphere Books, U.K. Page 78.
4. Bennett Cerf, THE LAUGH'S ON ME (1959). Reprinted by permission of Doubleday, a division of Bantam, Doubleday, Dell Publishing Group Inc., New York. Page 353-354.
5. Jewish Jokes for the JOHN. Kanrom Inc., New York. Pages 124-125.
8. Leon Harris, FINE ART OF POLITICAL WIT. Reprinted by permission of MacMillan Publishing Company, New York.
9. Bennett Cerf, THE LIFE OF THE PARTY (1956). Reprinted by permission of Doubleday, a division of Bantam, Doubleday, Dell Publishing Group Inc., New York. Pages 88-89.

IX CHUCKLES IN THE VATICAN

1. TIME MAGAZINE — January 26, 1959.
2. Kenneth Edwards, I WISH I'D SAID THAT! (1976). Reprinted by permission of Blackie & Son Limited, U.K. Page 58.
3-5. Rev Fr Mauricio Rufino, A VADEMECUM OF STORIES (1972). Reprinted by permission of St. Paul Publications, Bandra, Bombay, India. Pages 238, 377, 702.
8-10. Patrick Mahony, BARBED WIT & MALICIOUS HUMOR (1956). Reprinted by permission of the Institute for the Study of Man, Washington. Page 181, 181-182, 182-183.

XI CHURCH COLLECTIONS & OFFERINGS

10-12. Cecil Hunt, LAUGHING GAS (1958). Reprinted by permission of Jaico Publications, Bombay, India. Pages 17, 69, 99.
15. Leslie & Bernice Flynn, HUMOROUS NOTES, QUOTES & ANECDOTES (1973). Reprinted by permission of Baker Book House, Grand Rapids. Page 36.
17. William R. Gerler, EXECUTIVE'S TREASURY OF HUMOR FOR EVERY OCCASION (1967). Reprinted by permission of William R. Gerler. Pages 197-198.
18. Steven Lukes & Itzhak Galnoor, NO LAUGHING MATTER (1985). Reprinted by permission of Routledge & Kegan Paul, U.K. Page 35.
19-20. 10,000 JOKES, TOASTS & STORIES by Lewis & Faye

Copeland. Copyright 1939,1940 by Lewis & Faye, Copeland and Copyright (c) 1965 by Doubleday, a division of Bantam, Doubleday, Dell Publishing Group Inc. Reprinted by permission of the publishers. Pages 514-515.

22. Tal D. Bonham. THE TREASURY OF CLEAN CHURCH JOKES (Nashville-Broadman Press, 1986). Page 80. All rights reserved. Used by permission.

27. Larry Wilde, LIBRARY OF LAUGHTER (1988). Reprinted by permission of Larry Wilde. Page 39.

31. Specified quote from the book THE SPEAKER'S HAND-BOOK OF HUMOUR BY Maxwell Droke. Copyright 1956 Maxwell Droke, Used by permission of the Publishers Harper & Row, Publishers Inc., New York.

XII CLERGY VS. CLERGY

2-3. Kenneth Edwards, I WISH I'D SAID THAT (1976). Reprinted by permission of Blackie & Son, Limited, U.K. Pages 56 and 63.

9. 10,000 JOKES, TOASTS & STORIES BY Lewis & Faye, Copeland. Copyright 1939, 1940 by Lewis & Faye Copeland and copyright (c) 1965 by Doubleday, a division of Bantam, Doubleday, Dell Publishing Group, Inc. Reprinted by permission of the publishers. Pages 517-518.

10. G.D. James, TALES WORTH TELLING. Published by Dr. G.D. James, Multi-media Ltd., P.O. Box 122, Epping, NSW, Australia.

12. Allan Laing, LAUGHTER & APPLAUSE. Reprinted with permission of Jaico Publishing House, 125 M.G. Road, Bombay 400 001.

XIII DENOMINATIONS

1. Marjorie Barrow, Mathilda Schirmer & Bennet Cerf, THE TREASURY OF HUMOR & TOASTMASTER'S HAND-BOOK. Published by Groiler Inc., New York. (Joke No. 193).

4-6. Tal D. Bonham. THE TREASURY OF CLEAN CHURCH JOKES (Nashville-Broadman Press, 1986). Pages 54 to 55 and page 60. All rights reserved. Used by permission.

8. Larry Wilde, LIBRARY OF LAUGHTER (1988). Reprinted by permission of Larry Wilde. Page 40.

XIV DOZING IN CHURCH

9. Leslie & Bernice Flynn, HUMOROUS NOTES, QUOTES &

ANECDOTES (1973). Reprinted by permission of Baker Book House. Page 144.

11. William R. Gerler, EXECUTIVE'S TREASURY OF HUMOR FOR EVERY OCCASION (1967). Reprinted by permission of William R. Gerler. Page 37.

12.14 10,000 JOKES, TOASTS & STORIES by Lewis & Faye Copeland. Copyright 1939, 1940 by Lewis & Faye Copeland and copyright (c) 1965 by Doubleday, a division of Bantam Doubleday, Dell Publishing Group, Inc., Reprinted by permission of the publishers. Pages 502, 507, 508-509.

22. Specified quote from the book THE SPEAKER'S HANDBOOK OF HUMOR BY Maxwell Droke. Copyright 1956 Maxwell Droke, Used by permission of the Publishers, Harper & Row, Publishers Inc., New York.

XV EPITAPHS

14-23. SAMUEL KLINGER, FUTURA PUBLICATIONS, London (1979).

XVI EVANGELISTS

1, 6-7. G. D. James, TALES WORTH TELLING, Published by Dr. G. D. James Multi-media Ltd. P.O. Box 122, Epping, N.S.W., 2121 Australia.

8-9. Murray Watts, Rolling in The Aisles (1987). Reprinted by permission of Monarch Publications Ltd., East Sussex, U.K. Pages 27 and 48.

12-13. Leslie & Bernice Flynn, HUMOROUS NOTES, QUOTES & ANECDOTES (1973). Reprinted by permission of Baker Book House, Grand Rapids, Michigan. Pages 123 and 171.

14. Patrick Mahony, BARBED WIT & MALICIOUS HUMOR (1956). Reprinted by permission of the Institute For The Study of Man, Washington. Page 179.

XVII EVE-TEASING

6. William R. Gerler, EXECUTIVE'S TREASURY OF HUMOR FOR EVERY OCCASION (1967). Reprinted by permission of William R. Gerler. Page 38.

12. Herbert V. Prochnow & Herbert V. Prochnow Jr., THE PUBLIC SPEAKER'S TREASURE CHEST (1977). Reprinted by permission of Thorsons Publishers Limited, U.K. Page 191.

15. Leslie & Bernice Flynn, HUMOROUS NOTES, QUOTES & ANECDOTES (1973). Reprinted by permission of Baker Book House Limited, Grand Rapids, Michigan. Page 46.

17. Larry Wilde, THE OFFICIAL RELIGIOUS/NOT SO RELI-
GIOUS JOKE BOOK. Reprinted by permission of Larry
Wilde. Page 13.

XVIII FUND-RAISING

1. Cecil Hunt, LAUGHING GAS (1958). Reprinted by permission of Jaico Publishing House, India. Page 56.

2. William R. Gerler, EXECUTIVE'S TREASURY OF HUMOR
FOR EVERY OCCASION (1967). Reprinted by permission
of William R. Gerler. Page 38.

6. 10,000 JOKES, TOASTS & STORIES by Lewis & Faye
Copeland. Copyright 1939, 1940 by Lewis & Faye Copeland
and copyright (c) 1965 by Doubleday, a division of Bantam,
Doubleday, Dell Publishing Group Inc. Reprinted by permission of the publishers.

8. Tal D. Bonham. THE TREASURY OF CLEAN CHURCH
JOKES. (Nashville, Broadman Press, 1986). Pages 29-30. All
rights reserved. Used by permission.

9. Larry Wilde, LIBRARY OF LAUGHTER (1988). Reprinted
by permission of Larry Wilde. Page 45.

10. Specified quote from the book THE SPEAKER'S HAND-
BOOK OF HUMOUR BY Maxwell Droke. Copyright 1956,
Maxwell Droke, Used by permission of the Publishers,
Harper & Row, Publishers Inc., New York.

XIX LAUGHTER IN HEAVEN

2-3. Murray Watts, ROLLING IN THE AISLES (1987). Reprinted by permission of Monarch Publications Limited,
East Sussex, U.K. Pages 111 and 127-128.

4. Peter Cagney, THE BOOK OF WIT & HUMOUR (1976).
Reprinted by permission of Thorsons Publishers Limited,
U.K. Page 207.

5. Steven Lukes & Itzhak Galnoor, NO LAUGHING MATTER
(1985) Reprinted by permission of Routledge & Kegan Paul,
U.K. Pages 98-99.

7. George Mikes, HUMOUR IN MEMORIAM. Reprinted by
permission of Routledge & Kegan Paul, U.K.

8. Bennett Cerf, LIFE OF THE PARTY (1956). Reprinted by
permission of Doubleday, a division of Bantam, Doubleday,
Dell Publishing Group, Inc., New York. Pages 89-90.

9. Steven Lukes & Itzhak Galnoor, NO LAUGHING MATTER
(1985). Reprinted by permission of Routledge & Kegan Paul,
U.K. Page 37.

12. Patrick Mahony, BARBED WIT & MALICIOUS HUMOR
(1956). Reprinted by permission of The Institute for The
Study of Man, Washington. Page 135.

XX **LIMERICKS**

1-4. THE WORLD'S BEST LIMERICKS (1951). Reprinted by permission of Peter Pauper Press, Inc., White Plains, New York.

XXI **MONKS & NUNS**

9. Murray Watts, ROLLING IN THE AISLES (1987). Reprinted by permission of Monarch Publications Limited, East Sussex. U.K. Page 64.

14-15. Larry Wilde, LIBRARY OF LAUGHTER (1988). Reprinted by permission of Larry Wilde. Pages 45 and 46.

XXII **PRAYERS**

1-10. E.C. Mackenzie, 14,000 QUIPS & QUOTES FOR WRITERS AND SPEAKERS (1980). Reprinted by permission of Baker Book House, Grand Rapids, Michigan.

12. Fred Trueman, YOU NEARLY HAD HIM THAT TIME! Reprinted by permission of Century Hutchinson Publishing Group Limited, U.K. Page 22.

13. RUGBY JOKES (1968). Reprinted by permission of Sphere Books, U.K.

14. William R. Gerler, EXECUTIVE'S TREASURY OF HUMOR FOR EVERY OCCASION (1967). Reprinted by permission of William R. Gerler. Page 196.

15. Reprinted with permission from July 1978 Reader's Digest. Copyright (c) 1978 by RDI Print & Publishing Private Limited.

17. Lewis & Faye Copeland, 10,000 JOKES, TOASTS & STORIES. Copyright 1939, 1940 by Lewis & Faye Copeland and copyright (c) 1965 by Doubleday, a division of Bantam, Doubleday, Dell Publishing Group Inc., Reprinted by permission of publishers.

18. Reprinted with permission from the June, 1982 Reader's Digest. Copyright (c) 1982 RDI Print & Publishing Private Limited.

19. Patrick Mahony, BARBED WIT & MALICIOUS HUMOR (1956). Reprinted by permission of The Institute For The Study of Man, Washington. Page 174.

22. Larry Wilde, LIBRARY OF LAUGHTER (1988). Reprinted by permission of Larry Wilde. Page 32.

25. From the book COMPLETE SPEAKER'S GALAXY OF FUNNY STORIES, JOKES AND ANECDOTES by WINSTON K. PENDLETON. (C) 1979. Used by permission of the

publishers, Parker Publishing Company, Inc., West Nyack, New York. Page 193.

26 & 27.   Allan M. Laing. LAUGHTER AND APPLAUSE (1957). Reprinted by permission of Jaico Publishing House, Bombay, India. Pages 41 and 116.

XXIII PULLING THE LAYMAN'S LEG

1. Rev Fr Mauricio Rufino, A VADEMECUM OF STORIES (1972). Reprinted by permission of St. Paul Publications, Bandra, Bombay, India. Page 404.

2-4. Leslie & Bernice Flynn, HUMOROUS NOTES, QUOTES & ANECDOTES (1973). Reprinted by permission of Baker Book House, Grand Rapids, Michigan. Pages 81, 82, 119.

6. 10,000 JOKES, TOASTS & STORIES by Lewis & Faye Copeland and copyright 1939, 1940 by Lewis & Faye Copeland. Copyright (c) 1965 by Doubleday, a division of Bantam Doubleday, Dell Publishing Group Inc., Reprinted by permission of the Publishers. Page 506.

7. Herbert V. Prochnow & Herbert V. Prochnow Jr., THE SPEAKER'S TREASURE CHEST (1977). Reprinted by permission of Thorsons Publishers Limited, U.K. Page 141.

XXV QUIPS & QUOTES

1-86. E.C. Mackenzie, 14,000 QUIPS & QUOTES FOR WRITERS & SPEAKERS (1988). Reprinted by permission of Baker Book House Limited, Grand Rapids, Michigan.

XXVI RELIGIOUS PUNS

1-20. Paul Jennings, PUN FUN (1980). Reprinted by permission of Century Hutchinson Publishing Group, U.K.

21. Leslie & Bernice Flynn, HUMOROUS NOTES, QUOTES & ANECDOTES (1973). Reprinted by permission of Baker Book House, Grand Rapids, Michigan. Page 84.

22. Reprinted with permission from the July 1986 Reader's Digest. Copyright (c) 1986 by RDI Print & Publishing Private Ltd.

24-25. Tal D. Bonham. THE TREASURY OF CLEAN CHURCH JOKES. (Nashville; Broadman Press, 1986) Pages 98 and 88. All rights reserved. Used by permission.

27. Larry Wilde, LIBRARY OF LAUGHTER (1988). Reprinted by permission of Larry Wilde. Page 44.

XXVII SAYING GRACE

2. 10000 JOKES, TOASTS & STORIES by Lewis & Faye

197

Copeland. Copyright 1939, 1940 by Lewis & Faye Copeland and copyright (c) 1965 by Doubleday, a division of Bantam, Doubleday, Dell Publishing Group Inc. Reprinted by permission of the publishers. Page 510.

3. Patrick Mahony, BARBED WIT & MALICIOUS HUMOR (1956). Reprinted by Permission of The Institute For The Study of Man, Washington. Page 93.

XXVIII SERMONS IN SMILES

1-2. Leslie & Bernice Flynn, HUMOROUS NOTES, QUOTES & ANECDOTES (1973). Reprinted by permission of Baker Book House, Grand Rapids, Michigan. Pages 137 & 135.

3. Herbert V. Prochnow & Herbert V. Prochnow Jr., QUOTATIONS FOR ALL OCCASIONS (1983). Reprinted by permission of Thorsons Publishers, U.K. Page 96.

7. Steven Lukes & Itzhak Galnoor, NO LAUGHING MATTER (1985). Reprinted by permission of Routledge & Kegan Paul, U.K. Page 136.

14. Larry Wilde, LIBRARY OF LAUGHTER (1988). Reprinted by permission of Larry Wilde. Page 44.

15. Larry Wilde. THE OFFICIAL RELIGIOUS/NOT SO RELIGIOUS JOKE BOOK — Reprinted by permission of Larry Wilde. Page 16.

XXIX SIN AND GIN

1. Israel H. Weisfeld, THE PULPIT TREASURY OF WIT & HUMOR (1950). Published by Prentice-Hall, Inc., New York. Pages 4-5.

2. Peter Cagney, THE BOOK OF WIT & HUMOUR (1976). Reprinted by permission of Thorsons Publishers Limited, U.K. Pages 326.

3. Excerpt from TREASURY OF HUMOR AND TOAST MASTERS HANDBOOK. Compiled by Marjorie Barrow, Mathilda Schirmer and Bennett Cerf (1983). Page 498.

4. Larry Wilde, THE LAST OFFICIAL IRISH JOKE BOOK. Reprinted by permission of Larry Wilde. Page 101.

5. THE SON OF RUGBY JOKES ( ). Reprinted by permission of Sphere Books, U.K.

6-7. William R. Gerler, EXECUTIVE'S TREASURY OF HUMOR FOR EVERY OCCASION (1967). Reprinted by permission of William R. Gerler. Pages 40 and 212.

11. Herbert V. Prochnow & Herbert V. Prochnow Jr., THE

PUBLIC SPEAKER'S TREASURE CHEST (1977). Reprinted by permission of Thorsons Publishers Limited, U.K. Page 164.

13. Patrick Mahony, BARBED WIT & MALICIOUS HUMOR (1956). Reprinted by permission of The Institute for the Study of Man, Washington. Page 180.

14. Tal D. Bonham. THE TREASURY OF CLEAN CHURCH JOKES (Nashville; Broadman Press, 1986). Page 89. All rights reserved. Used by permission.

16. Larry Wilde, LIBRARY OF LAUGHTER (1988). Reprinted by permission of Larry Wilde. Pages 38 and 48.

17. THE SON OF RUGBY JOKES. Reprinted by permission of Sphere Books, U.K.

XXX SPOONERISMS

3. Cecil Hunt, LAUGHING GAS (1958). Reprinted by permission of Jaico Publishing House, India. Page 97.

6. Larry Wilde, THE OFFICIAL RELIGIOUS/NOT SO RELIGIOUS JOKE BOOK (1988). Page 9. Reprinted by permission of Larry Wilde.

7. Paul Jennings, PUN FUN (1980). Reprinted by permission of Century Hutchinson Publishing Group, U.K.

XXXI SUNDAY SCHOOLS

1. Herbert V. Prochnow & Herbert V. Prochnow Jr., QUOTATIONS FOR ALL OCCASIONS (1983). Reprinted by permission of Thorsons Publishers Limited, U.K. Page 535.

2. LAUNDERED LIMERICKS (1960). Reprinted by permission of Peter Pauper Press, White Plains, New York.

4. Bennett Cerf, THE LAUGH'S ON ME (1959). Reprinted by permission of Doubleday, a division of Bantam Doubleday Dell Publishing Group Inc. Page 352.

5. Herbert V. Prochnow & Herbert V. Prochnow Jr., QUOTATIONS FOR ALL OCCASIONS (1983). Reprinted by permission of Thorsons Publishers Limited U.K. Page 93.

6. Reprinted by permission of Good News, Economic Press Inc. and also reprinted with permission from the July 1978 Reader's Digest.

10. Israel H. Weisfeld, THE PULPIT. TREASURY OF HUMOR & WIT (1950). Prentice — Hall Inc., New York. Pages 19-20.

XXXII TEN COMMANDMENTS

9. William R. Gerler, EXECUTIVE'S TREASURY OF HUMOR FOR EVERY OCCASION (1967). Reprinted by permission of William R. Gerler. Page 212.

10 & 11. Leslie & Bernice Flynn, HUMOROUS NOTES, QUOTES & ANECDOTES (1973). Reprinted by permission of Baker Book House, Grand Rapids, Michigan. Page 153.

13. Specified quote from the book THE SPEAKER'S HANDBOOK OF HUMOUR BY Maxwell Droke. Copyright 1956, Maxwell Droke, Used by permission of the Publishers, Harper & Row, Publishers Inc., New York.

XXXIII VERSE & WORSE

9. FUN AND NONSENSE. Edited by Louis Untermeyer. Published by William Collins Sons & Co. (London) (1970).

18. Patrick Mahony, BARBED WIT & MALICIOUS HUMOR (1970). Reprinted by permission of The Institute For Study of Man, Washington. Pages 177-178.

XXXIV WIT & SARCASM

1. Herbert V. Prochnow & Herbert V. Prochnow Jr., QUOTATIONS FOR ALL OCCASIONS (1983). Reprinted by permission of Thorsons Publishers Limited, U.K. Pages 316-317.

3. Peter Cagney, THE BOOK OF WIT & HUMOUR (1976). Reprinted by permission of Thorsons Publishers, U.K. Page 202.

4. Alfred Noyes, TWO WORLDS FOR MEMORY. Reprinted by permission of Hugh Noyes, Isle of Wight.

10. Patrick Mahony, BARBED WIT & MALICIOUS HUMOR (1956). Reprinted by permission of The Institute For The Study of Man, Washington. Pages 180-181.

14. Herbert V. Prochnow & Herbert V. Prochnow Jr., QUOTATIONS FOR ALL OCCASIONS (1983). Reprinted by permission of Thorsons Publishers Limited, U.K. Page 242.

15. Tal D. Bonham. THE TREASURY OF CLEAN CHURCH JOKES (Nashville, Broadman Press, 1986. Pages 25-26. All rights reserved. Used by permission.

11. Garden Lang: MR. JUSTICE AVORY (Herbert Jenkins, 1935).

12. From the book COMPLETE SPEAKER'S GALAXY OF FUNNY STORIES, JOKES AND ANECDOTES. By WINSTON K. PENDLETON. (C) 1979. Used by permission of the publisher, Parker Publishing Company, Inc., West Nyack, NY. Page 164.

13. Excerpt from BRIEF LIFE by Cecil Whitley. Reprinted by permission of MacMillan Publishers Limited, London.

14. Allan M. Laing: LAUGHTER & APPLAUSE (1957). Reprinted by permission of Jaico Publishing House, Bombay. Page 22.

15. Specified quote from the book SPEAKER'S HANDBOOK OF HUMOR by Maxwell Droke. Copyright (c) 1956 by Maxwell Droke. Used by permission of publishers, Harper & Row, Publishers Inc., NY. Page 27.

16. Joey Adam's ETHNIC HUMOR (1975). Manor Book Inc. NY. Page 189.

17. Excerpt from THE TREASURY OF HUMOR AND TOASTMASTER'S HANDBOOK. Compiled by Marjorie Barrow, Mathilda Schirmer and Bennett Cerf. Published by Grolier Inc. NY. Joke No. 191.

18. Bennett Cerf: THE LAUGH'S ON ME. Reprinted by permission of Doubleday, a division of Bantam, Doubleday, Dell Publishing Group Inc. Pages 350-351.

19. Excerpt from QUOTES & ANECDOTES by Anthony P. Castle. Reprinted by permission of St Paul Publications, Bombay. Page 326.

20. 10,000 JOKES, TOASTS & STORIES by Lewis & Faye Copeland. Copyright 1939, 1940 by Lewis & Faye Copeland. Copyright (c) 1965 by Doubleday, a division of Bantam, Doubleday, Dell Publishing Group Inc. Reprinted by permission of the publishers. Page 504.

21. Excerpt from THE PUBLIC SPEAKER'S TREASURE CHEST by Herbert V. Prochnow and Herbert V. Prochnow Jr. Reprinted by permission of Thorsons Publishers Limited, UK. Pages 81-82.

Every effort has been made to trace the copyright owners. In a few instances, I have been unable to trace the copyright holders despite several attempts. If I have inadvertently omitted any acknowledgement which should have been made, I crave the indulgence of the author or publisher and will make acknowledgement in future editions.

(JUDSON K. CORNELIUS)